Jesus Goes to McDonald's

Jesus Goes to McDonald's
Theology and Consumer Society

Luiz Alexandre Solano Rossi

Foreword by
Norman K. Gottwald

WIPF & STOCK · Eugene, Oregon

JESUS GOES TO MCDONALD'S
Theology and Consumer Society

Copyright © 2011 Luiz Alexandre Solano Rossi. All rights reserved. Except for brief quotations in critical publications or reviews, no part of this book may be reproduced in any manner without prior written permission from the publisher. Write: Permissions, Wipf and Stock Publishers, 199 W. 8th Ave., Suite 3, Eugene, OR 97401.

Wipf and Stock Publishers
199 W. 8th Ave., Suite 3
Eugene, OR 97401

www.wipfandstock.com

ISBN 13: 978-1-61097-253-6

Cataloging-in-Publication data:

Rossi, Luiz Alexandre Solano.

Jesus goes to MacDonald's : theology and consumer society / Luiz Alexandre Solano Rossi, with a foreword by Norman K. Gottwald.

xviii + 122 p. ; 23 cm. Includes bibliographical references.

ISBN 13: 978-1-61097-253-6

1. Bible. O.T. Job—Criticism, interpretation, etc. 2. Wealth—Religious aspects—Christianity. 3. Capitalism—Religious aspects—Protestant churches. 4. Poverty—Religious aspects—Christianity. I. Gottwald, Norman K. (Norman Karol), 1926– II. Title.

BR1018.U66 R55 2011

Manufactured in the U.S.A.

To the beloved:
Lourdes, Márcia, Nina, Vilma, Cidinha, Dalva, Maria do Carmo, Andréia, Izaura, Itamar, Haroldo, Martins, Milton, José Roberto (*in memorian*).

Contents

Foreword by Norman K. Gottwald / ix
Acknowledgments / xi
Introduction / xiii

1 The Empire Fights Back: Job and the Origin of the Poor's Suffering / 1
2 Theology and Anti-Theology in the Book of Job / 16
3 The Theology of Prosperity / 46
4 Building Solidarity on the Road of Defeat / 78
   Conclusion / 115

Bibliography / 119

Foreword

THIS ARRESTING WORK IS far more substantial than the "catchy" title may imply. The actual topic of the book is the impact of consumerism on the church and theology. This theme has been developed by others, but Luiz Alexandre Solano Rossi has managed a novel approach on three counts. First, it treats Job's struggle against "the theology of reward" as the prototype of today's struggle against the "theology of prosperity." Second, it shows in considerable detail how the theology of reward has driven the rapid growth of Pentecostalism in the author's home state of Brazil. Third, he shows how the working premises of the fast food industry closely parallel much current theology that has capitulated to the allure and peril of consumerism.

Not since Gustavo Gutierrez's *On Job* has there been such a compelling reading of the Book of Job as a literary mirror of oppressive socioeconomic and political conditions. The author convincingly portrays the Book of Job as a protest against the depressing effects of imperial Persian rule in postexilic Judah, which he sees as the stimulus for the theology of reward so fiercely castigated by Job. The exposition of Brazilian Pentecostalism goes beyond the frequent claim that people are drawn by its emotional spontaneity by fixing on the Pentecostal promise that those who believe can expect to achieve payoff in economic prosperity. Finally, "the McDonaldization of society" becomes a lucid metaphor for showing how theology has become slick, superficial, and decidedly unhealthy. This invasion of church and theology by the capitalist drive to consume is illuminated under the rubrics of efficiency, calculability, predictability, and control.

The publication of Luiz Alexandre S. Rossi's book is a clear demonstration that Latin American liberation theology continues to produce solid biblical exegesis, trenchant social critique, and riveting theological reflection that enrich the worldwide church.

Norman K. Gottwald
Professor at Pacific School of Religion, Berkeley, CA

Acknowledgments

DURING THE PERIOD I was researching and writing this book I was privileged to meet many people who eventually became not only friends but also valuable supporters in the task of completing this book. To them I express my deepest gratitude.

Firstly, my acknowledgments to the Global Research Institute, for their kindness in granting me a scholarship that made it possible to turn 2006 into a sabbatical year at Fuller Theological Seminary, Pasadena, California. My sincere gratitude to Dr. Walther Hansen and Dr. Jehu Hanciles from Global Research Institute, who not only allowed me to enjoy a year of intense research, but also provided my family and me with the support and care for all our needs.

I am especially grateful to my friend Enock of Assis for being ahead, leading my steps to obtain the scholarship indication, despite the obstacles that occurred during the process, and for his original suggestion to the title of this book. The friendship and stimulating presence of this great friend was extremely fruitful and productive.

I would also like to thank the many friends I made when I lived in Pasadena. They all became an extension of my own family, especially the Melo's family: Jairton, Christina, Anna, and Philip. Their friendship and caring are indelibly engraved in my heart.

My list of thanks would be incomplete without expressing my gratitude to my wife, Eliane, for helping in writing the book manuscript in English (a requirement of the Global Research Institute) and my beloved sons, Matthew and Barbara, who also were supporters during this time.

Introduction

THE CONTEMPORARY SOCIETY LIVES under the intense flux of ambition for "more"—more income, more assets, more success, more consumer goods—without limit. This phenomenon can be called consumerism or a consumer society. A consumer society is best described as one in which the possession and use of an increasing number and variety of goods and services is the principal aspiration and the surest perceived route to an individual's happiness, social status, and personal success. It is a cultural phenomenon that somehow animates vast numbers of people. The effect of consumerism is that the desire for growth becomes obsessive and idolatrous, the scale of growth becomes the excessive form that many people use to get advantages at the expense of others, and the means for growth become filled with greed, exploitation, and injustice.

If we attentively look at humanity, we will see that it is facing one of its major crises: the increasing polarization between the rich and the poor. Economic data reveal ethical scandals that should bother us, since not everyone can have "more"; the majority is condemned to have "less" and survive with "less." The opportunity to buy and thereby to have access to the restricted circle of those who own "more" is not available to everyone. The exclusion zone has been well built and delimited. Buying is the only way to salvation! The impact of this pathology is not restricted to the individual but is extended to the whole society. Before the dehumanizing situation faced by the majority, the relatively rich ones thank God for the advantage of being rich as if it was a blessing of God. Actually, the economic structures are the ones that reward the rich and keep the poor in poverty. And they are manifestations of the system and not just personal evil.

I use the Book of Job as a reference to show how theology can also be related to this practice of reward. I call it "the theology of reward."

According to this theology, God gives wealth to some and poverty to others. This way, the rich are rich and continue like that because they are upright; and the poor are poor and possibly will continue like that because they did not trust in God's justice, or rather, they are sinners. Job tries to give a response to the fundamental questions present in that biblical text regarding this kind of theology. Job's experience proclaims from its very beginning that there is no correlation between sin and suffering; between virtue and reward.

In our postmodern ecclesiastic environment, one of the possible expressions for the theology of reward is "Prosperity Theology." This theology declares that God's plan for the human beings is to make them happy, blessed, healthy, and prosperous; in other words, to make them very "successful" persons. One problem with this theology lies in its claim that if an individual is not financially successful, healthy, and happy, the reason is that he or she lacks faith, does not fulfill what the Bible says about the divine promises, is in some way involved with Satan, or is living a sinful life.

Such logic is hard for us to break free from because we tend to think from or with the logic of the victors. From this logic, the Christian's quotidian should be integrally marked by words like wealth, health, power, and success that describe victory over the evil forces. All these words are seen in bright theological colors to indicate that many times we witness a theology being constructed from the perspective of the victors, who impose their logic of power in a consumerist society. The theology of prosperity shows that theology is not immune to the virus of consumption as it constantly stimulates us to look for the signals of God's presence in our income, our big "temples," our relations with prestigious people, our growth statistics, and in external appearance of wealth.

However, we have to live with the consequences of a sort of theology that produces fragmentation and exclusion and that helps to build a situation in which the world is being re-ordered into winners and losers. Those who are able to access the world market and reap the benefits can join increasingly interconnected global elite, while the rest struggle on the margins. We may say that the current world is divided between those who worship in comfortable contentment and those who, enslaved by the world's economic injustice, suffer and die.

Confronted with this scenario, in this book I present a counter-discourse to the discourse of the theology of prosperity. How could theology affirm the sovereignty of victory in a society of defeated people? How can we say that we believe Jesus is the Lord over all life and at the same time create a theology that denies the promise of a life of plenty to the world? Theology should not stimulate a religiosity *of* victors *for* victors because it is an excluding religiosity. A theology that proclaims prosperity and victory as signals of God's presence in a society marked by poverty, suffering, and failure has no relevance as a theological discourse for the churches.

However, the healthy theology that comes from most of the biblical texts is presented as a gospel testimony and thus a testimony of life. We cannot separate theology from life or we risk condemning it to be antitheology. Without this insight, a theological discourse is nothing other than a visionary experience; and, without this sensibility, a theologian is no one other than a visionary charlatan, and his theology, a pure illusion.

We must think of theology as a voice for the voiceless. We cannot deny the poor their right to a theological discourse that defends them and that is inclusive in the construction of a new society. It is necessary to look at the history of humanity as a starting point for a theological reflection that protects the right of the poor to survive in a society that excludes them, by creating peripheries.

One of the tasks of theology and, consequently, the theologian's task is to unmask the incestuous relation between capital and profit. Global economic justice is essential to the integrity of our faith and to the construction of healthy theologies in a society marked by the suffering of the poor. No economic system that produces injustice and dishonest dealing can be blessed or legitimized or tolerated in the name of God. Wealth and success are not necessarily an expression of blessing. On the contrary, they can be understood as a mark of a "social predator." The words of Jesus in Matt 6:24, "You cannot serve God and Mamnon," are now more important than ever, because our global economic system focuses primarily on money, and the ideology behind it gives priority to the accumulation of wealth. I remember that one of the documents of the World Alliance of Reformed Churches (Gana, 2004) whose title is "*Covenanting for Justice in the Economy and the Earth*" is a clear challenge for the churches to think about oppression of the global economic system.

A church that has a healthy theology consequently presents itself as a non-conformist church, a prophetic community. It makes sense to say that God calls his people to be signs of shalom, the vanguard of God's eschatological community, a community of cultural changes. A healthy theology calls us to live with this vision and the people of God are given the responsibility of transmitting and sustaining that vision as well as making manifest its meaning.

The theology that is in my heart and that I try to describe in this book is a theology that fights and teaches others to fight for the *victims'* lives, for their right to a worthy life. It is a theology that produces a sense that should be found and lived even when there is no guarantee of victory. We need to stop justifying our privileges and to start discovering, unmasking, and denouncing the mechanisms of oppression that make and keep people poor. We need to examine our theologies and ask whether Christ is presented as liberator of the oppressed or as a champion of an unjust *status quo,* and whether our gospel is good news to the poor or only a rationalization for the rich. Finally, I try to show here that theology must have a prophetic function and serve as a critique of the ideology of consumerism.

Four chapters constitute this book. The first is an attempt to recover, as much as possible, the background of the biblical text that describes Job's experiences; in other words, the context of the Persian Empire. It is in this context that I localize Job. His experience is an impressive circumstance in which an individual case becomes a typical one, and it reflects the inequality of the community that struggles in historical conditions that seem to cast doubt upon the justice of God. So, it is important and necessary to try to recover, as far as we are able, the socio-economical environment where the Book of Job was written, as well as the theological environment of the various speeches present in the book. In this sense, Job addresses God and describes the human condition through his own example. Thus, we should not see Job as an individual and lonely person; we should not look at him as an exception. On the contrary, he is the spokesman of a history and society that are full of contradictions. His outcry is not the cry of a lone man, but the first outcry of a series—a series that includes our own laments. Throughout history these howls of protest have been united in order to express that pain, which, though intense, can be overcome in solidarity. Job's painful outcry is a clear warning for us to turn our eyes to his experience if we truly wish to meet God and to hear a theological voice that is relevant to our days.

In the second chapter I engage two completely different kinds of theology, although many times we may think that they are equal. I bring Job's friends together to offer a so-called "official theological speech" that comes from a theology that makes impossible any kind of autonomous reflection when it tries to keep the social order. Job's theological speeches, on the other hand, are constructed on the periphery from the perspective of those who suffer economically and theologically. The story revealed with Job's experience is presumably addressed to the people who owned lands and stocks but had lost their possessions. Their loss was caused by internal and external factors. It is important to notice that both kinds of factor are instruments of dehumanization and we may even say that they were the most penetrating instruments in people's skin. It is before this alienating scenario that the official theology was born. It was born with the desire to teach peasants, by means of catechesis, to have patience—Job's patience—to accept everything and, mainly, remain silent. So, the picture we see is deeply murky and grey. The "official theology" was set in place in an agrarian crisis when the produce of agricultural activity started being directed to the international market and no longer to the peasant's subsistence. It was a time when people stopped planting merely for their subsistence in order to plant for the commerce. People, then, faced a double taxation: tribute charged by the Persian Empire and tribute charged by the Temple in Jerusalem.

The third chapter sets us before the speech of the theology of prosperity. It asserts that this theology stimulates consumption since such consumption is understood to be an indubitable evidence of God's presence in the believer's life. Prosperity theology is very much at home in a consumer society. As such, I try to demonstrate that theology undergoes a reformulation of four dimensions just like the McDonaldization process: efficiency, calculability, predictability, and control. After that transformation it ceases to be an inclusive theology that defends life and instead becomes a simulacrum of theology that helps to construct walls that inevitably remove the poor from a fair world. As a result, the modern human being becomes the fruit of divisions and a controllable target for the powerful; he develops an individualistic and materialist character, unaware of the social reality that surrounds him. When the theology of prosperity stimulates the believer to consume, it is reinforcing in him such a character, instead of transforming him into a more conscious and solidary person. This way, communitarian practices have been replaced by individual well-being.

In the fourth and last chapter, I try to find God's social place and show that the concepts of victory and success are useless to elaborate any kind of theology. When the theology of prosperity sets itself under the same umbrella where capital and profit are sheltered, it turns into a theology of desire that stimulates consumption as criteria to define what a human being is. In this sense, theology is no longer understood as an instrument for an individual to reach self-accomplishment. Instead, it is transformed into an instrument through which an individual enters the consumption market, feels accomplished, and finally gets his certificate of human being. Theology comes to be seen as the fuel that feeds the fire of desire. In this sort of theology, the voice of consumerism is the voice of God.

1

The Empire Fights Back
Job and the Origin of the Poor's Suffering

INTRODUCTION: JOB AS EVERYMAN

JOB IS A LEGITIMATE representative of all human beings. His experience is that of an individual sufferer whose story becomes a typical one that reflects the inequality of the community struggling in historical conditions that seem to put in doubt the justice of God. Therefore it is important and necessary to try to recover as much as possible the socio-economic environment in which the Book of Job was written, as well as the theological environment of the various speeches presented in the book. In this sense, Job addresses God and describes the human condition through his own example. Thus, we should not see Job as a solitary person; we should not look at him as an exception. On the contrary, he is the spokesman of a history and a society that are full of contradictions. His outcry is not the cry of a lone man, but the first outcry of many—including our own—that throughout history have been joined in such a way as to reveal that pain, even intense pain, can be overcome with solidarity. Job's painful outcry is a clear warning for us to look at his experience if we truly wish to meet God and to find a theological speech that is relevant to our days.

The author of the Book of Job deliberately created a character who is not an Israelite, does not live in Israel, seldom refers to God as Yahweh, and makes no allusions to the history of Israel's covenant with God. *Job is everyman*; his innocent suffering is a challenge to retributive ideas of

God's justice, especially favored in exilic and postexilic meditations on the catastrophe of 586 BCE. It is possible to establish the date of this book between 450 and 350 BCE of postexilic period, during the domination of the Persian Empire.[1]

EXPLORING JUDEA IN THE PERSIAN PERIOD—BACKGROUND TO JOB

Persian Politics—The Big Picture

Unfortunately, the sources of information concerning Jewish daily life during that period are sparse. However, the writings preserved under the names of Ezra and Nehemiah, and possibly also some late addenda to prophetic books, do allow some conclusions. Also, according to Gerstenberger, "the Jewish legal documents and letters found in Elephantine, an island in the Nile River, offer a glimpse into the life of that particular Jewish military colony in Persian service."[2]

The Persians were an Indo-European people who had settled in Parsa by the sixth century BCE, in the mountainous lands, east of the Persian Gulf's northern coastline. At that time, the Persians were vassals of the Medes, another Indo-European group that occupied the Iranian north plateau of the Zagros Mountains and established their capital at Ecbatana. In 550 BCE Cyrus (who began his career in 560/559 BCE) rebelled against his overlord, the aging Median warrior-king Astyages. Cyrus successful uprising won for him the territories of the Medes and provided him with a substantial pool of army recruits. Cyrus's next target was the Lydian kingdom of Croesus, an ally of Babylonia. In 546 BCE Cyrus effectively destroyed Lydian sovereignty by a surprise winter assault on Sardis.

With a combination of hard combat, self-interested leniency, and propaganda, Cyrus brought the Greek cities on the Ionian coast of Asia Minor into his realm. Cyrus briefly turned his attention to his eastern front, but soon aimed his military might at the principal unconquered power in his path: Babylonia and its king, Nabonidus. As neighbors of the Medes and formal allies of Croesus, the Babylonians (and their Jewish populations) could be hardly unaware of Cyrus's relentless accumulation of territory. While the Persian conquest of Babylonia in 539 BCE was not

---

1. On the dating of Job see Schokel and Díaz, *Job: comentario teológico y literario*.

2. Gerstenberger, *Leviticus*, 7.

the quick and easy victory suggested by some of the sources, the capital Babylon fell without any casualties. Cyrus's success is credited to military acumen, to judicious bribery, and to an energetic publicity campaign waged throughout Babylonia that portrayed him as a lenient and religiously tolerant overlord.

With the reign of Darius, (522–485 BCE), Persian and Jewish history takes a new turn. To consolidate his control and to further integrate the political and social order of conquered territories into his imperial system, Darius embarked on a series of administrative reforms. His empire was divided in regions called satrapies that were administrated by satraps. This basic political administrative unit, around which the empire worked, had its origin with the Medo king Quiaxares. Nevertheless, this model was improved by Darius I[3] and gave to that large empire its definitive organization. According to Cazelles,[4] at the end of Darius's reign, it was possible to count thirty-one satrapies, but Herodotus, by 450 BC, knew only twenty satrapies, each one with one satrap who was usually a Medo or Persian noble, nominated by the king. (Though absolute precision eludes us. Cazelles points that in inscription of Darius the Great in Behistun twenty-three provinces that would turn out satrapies were numbered. He adds that on the trilingual structural text found in Suza—that would have been written in Egypt by 495 BC—twenty-four satrapies were counted.)

The satraps were quite autonomous and the local rulers were dependent on them. In spite of that, military commanders nominated by the king rigorously supervised them. These commanders were responsible for a complex bureaucracy and for a system of itinerant inspectors who also had to account to the king.[5] They were called "the king's eyes" and supervised the tax payment as well as the way the rebellions were controlled. Inside their well-defined regions, they had more power than the satraps and also established the tax value that each dominated region should pay. Even when the king was absent, people knew the commanders would inform him about their actions.

Judah was a "beyond the river" or a "Trans-Euphrates" satrapy category, that included the group of Syria and Palestine. As Gottwald points

---

3. Tunnermann, *As reformas de Neemias*, 20.
4. Cazelles, *História*, 218.
5. Bright, *História*, 447.

out, it is not clear whether Judah had the *status* of a province, separated since the beginning, or whether it was subjected to the authority of the Province of Samaria, at least until Nehemiah's period.[6]

Darius's organization judicially equalized all the satrapies. It meant that all of them—Judah included—should pay tribute. Judah was now just a small province or sub-province of a gigantic empire that virtually dominated all the world known by the peoples of the ancient Near East.

Tribute—Funding the Empire

Tunnermann's analysis about that time sheds some light on the issue and helps us to understand the increasing level of exploitation. He notices that, during Nebuchadnezzar's reign, the interest taxes were around 10 percent per year and rose over 20 percent during Cyrus's and Cambyses's reigns. During the fifth century, the taxes reached levels of 40 to 50 percent per year and in Judea the interest tax was about 60 percent per year.[7] He also claims that the increase of slave commerce in the Mediterranean in this period was a direct consequence of the debts caused by the Persian tributary system.[8]

Herodotus, the Greek historian, gives us a good example of the heavy burden of tribute laid upon the shoulders of the peasants. His account shows that Judea had to pay 350 silver talents of tribute to the emperor each year.[9] We know that one talent was worth about 6,000 denary and one denary was equivalent to one day-work payment. So, one talent was worth 6,000 days of work. As a result, paying a tribute of 350 talents was equivalent to giving to the Persian Empire the 2,100,000 days of work!

Tribute was the mechanism the Empire used to extract part of people's life. With the tribute, almost all the satrapies had to pay fixed taxes on cereals, horses, mules, sheep, weapons, eunuchs, young men and women, and food to the imperial troops settled in the satrapy.[10] Besides the direct tribute, there were the customs taxes, such as harbor taxes, and commercial taxes that people had to pay to navigate in the channels and use the port areas. The Persian Empire also had the power to recruit

6. Gottwald, *Introdução*, 402.
7. Tunnermann, *As reformas*, 55.
8. Ibid., 27.
9. Kippenberg, *Religião*, 48.
10. Dadamaev, *Political*, 180.

people for agricultural or construction work. As Neh 5:14–18 indicates, the dominated people also had to support the satrapy and the province chancellery.

Persian Rule in Judea

According to Hayes and Miller, the province (*medinah*) of Judea was small.[11] This term—*medinah*—is found in Imperial Aramaic and was used in the Persian chancelleries to designate a small or large province. However, Judea could hardly have an area larger than 2,500 or 3,500 km2. The province was divided in nine districts (*pelek*), under the command of an official called "*sar*" (Neh 3:14). Each district was sub-divided into half districts commanded by an administrative official, also called "sar" (Neh 3:9). This new administrative system brought bitter consequences to the native people as it eliminated the importance of the old clans and the families as local units. It is not possible to know what their population levels were, but this was an agrarian economy and the majority still worked on the land, even those living in cities. During the Persian domination, most of the Province of Judea was located in a mountainous area. Only part of its northern area reached the Jordan prairie. There, through irrigation, it was possible to cultivate crops, while in the mountainous area the predominant cultivation was dependent on rains. This kind of cultivation yielded less profit since regular irrigation was not possible.[12] In spite of being considered large, the city of Jerusalem was not sufficiently populated to feel safe against the attacks of neighboring peoples. At that time, Jerusalem population has been estimated at about 10,000 people.[13]

Ezra 2:63 mentions Judah's governor and calls him *tiršātâ*, a Persian title that probably means "Excellency." The term *pehâ*, also used in Ezra, is an Imperial Aramaic term designating a governor either of a large satrapy or of a small province.[14] In Ezra, this title is given to both Sheshbazzar and Zerubbabel (Ezra 3:2; 5:13–16; 6:3–5). Later, this title is used by Nehemiah of himself (Neh 12:26) and also of the governors (*pahôt*) who had held this position before him (Neh 5:15). The Persian title *tiršātâ* is also used by Nehemiah (Neh 7:65). According to

11. Hayes and Miller, *Israelite*, 522.
12. Kippenberg, *Religião*, 42.
13. Hayes and Miller, *Israelite*, 522.
14. Ibid., 510.

this information Judah had Persian governors from Sheshbazzar's and Zerubbabel's periods until Nehemiah's.

When the interests of Persia government were not directly involved, the province was a unit that governed itself. The governor had the task of collecting the tribute to be sent to the real treasury. Another responsibility of the governor was to represent people at the assembly, which in Judea was constituted exclusively by Jews, known as "sons of exile" (Ezra 10:7). Foreigners living in the country did not belong to this unit known as *qāhāl* (Ezra 10:12). In this assembly, we can find different terms to name the leaders, such as: noble men (*horîm*), elders (*zĕqēnîm*), chiefs (*sarîm*), magnates (*addîrîm*) and the heads of families (*hā'ābôt*).

The nature of the Persian administration of Palestine as well as the place of that system in Samaria and Judah are still obscure. Because Persia took over the Babylonian empire at one stroke by conquering Babylon it is supposed that, in the early years of Persian control, the Babylonian provincial and sub-provincial framework remained in place. For instance: the Persian administrative center nearest Jerusalem was in Mizpah: "Next to them, repairs were made by men from Gibeon and Mizpah—Melatiah of Gibeon and Jadon of Meronoth—places under the authority of the governor of Trans-Euphrates" (Neh 3:7), formerly the seat of the Babylonian authorities (2 Kgs 25:9).

Persian Tolerance?

The historical records indicate that the "civilized" Persians were just as capable of destroying sanctuaries and deporting peoples as their supposedly strong-handed predecessors, the Babylonians. The most judicious approach is to acknowledge both the tyrannical and the tolerant policies. According to Leith,[15] texts dating to the reigns of later Persian kings do confirm a pattern of Persian religious tolerance and noninterference in the cultural traditions of subject peoples. However—and this is essentially a Persian innovation—the temples were obliged to pay taxes to the Persians, in kind. Food, livestock, wool, and laborers were regularly required by the Persians from their subordinate temple communities, which were expected to support local officials of the empire with food rations. It was not high-minded respect for individual peoples, ethnic groups, and foreign religions that motivated Persian policy. Rather, Persian policy was

15. Leith, *Israel*, 285.

driven by enlightened self-interest. By reconciling the central power to local subjects, the Persians strengthened their empire.

Certainly, a violent process of domination and exploitation marked the Persian period. All subjugated peoples had to pay tribute to maintain the central Persian power. That is to say that the world-powerful Persia engaged in healthy exploitation of subjugated people. According to Briant,[16] the method Darius used to settle the boundaries of the districts and their tribute is very interesting: "for administrative purposes, neighboring nations were joined in a single unit; outlying people were considered to belong to this nation or that, according to convenience." From the perspective of tribute, the peoples of a province were grouped together and contributed together. A district was first and foremost a combination of neighboring peoples. Darius' principle of tribute was simple: every community in the empire had to turn over part of its production to the king of kings (i.e., himself). This included the less-known peoples, such as the inhabitants of the islands in the Persian Gulf, the place where the king used to send those who had been displaced from their homes during the war.

Metzger, however, agrees with the older vision of Persian politics as manifesting "great-tolerance."[17] In doing so, he does not permit a deeper analysis of the Persian society and its relationship with the dominated peoples. In his book, we find no hint of any antagonistic relations between the subjugated peoples and the Empire. Tunnermann offers a somewhat more balanced perspective. After emphasizing that Persia was the first world empire that proclaimed itself tolerant and benevolent in its treatment of tribes and conquered peoples, he adds that "tolerance can not be confused with looseness. The Persians had a very strict administrative organization."[18] Besides this, through a sharp system of communication and espionage, excellent military equipment, the construction and maintenance of imperial roads, mail service, coinage, and with only one official language, the Persian Empire enforced considerable uniformity and became a huge and viable political empire.[19]

---

16. Briant, *From Cyrus*, 393.
17. Metzger, *História*, 132.
18. Tunnermann, *As reformas*, 13–14.
19. Ibid., 14.

Tension in Judah and the Place of Theology

According to Gerstenberger, the Jews' economic and political dependence did not prevent social tensions from growing or urbanization and stratification from advancing among the Jewish people.[20] While a few members of the Jewish cultic community were able to amass fortunes and obtain influential positions through their collaborations with the Persians, the mass of population had to make do with a more or less unstable existence. For Briant, the local elite were closely linked to the imperial elite (or part of it). This is probably one of the reasons for the long life enjoyed by local dynasties and, more generally, client regimes: "the Persian authority was to some extent concealed behind the screen of the local gentry, who were entrusted with levying tribute and taxes locally, with the result that any possible discontent on the part of the peasants was aimed at these gentry (as seen in Nehemiah's Judah)."[21]

Against this social backdrop, it is quite understandable that especially the poorer classes among these inhabitants turned to religious life with increased fervor. In building upon Yahweh's intervention on behalf of the poor and oppressed, the postexilic Old Testament texts betray something about the structure of the Jewish communities during this period. These communities consisted to a large extent of the economically weak ones; that is, families who had gone bankrupt as a result of the enormous tribute pressure, or that were in risk of losing their economic independence. At the beginning and during much of the Persian period, Judah was poorer, less populous, and more isolated than the surrounding territories. So, Job presents himself not only as an individual, but also as one of the many people that had lost their flocks, their lands and even their sons and daughters.

It is possible to notice that the impoverishment process happened in a double form. The first form of exploitation was external—the Persian Empire that dominated Judea during that period. The second form of exploitation was internal—the rich traders linked to the high priests' families who controlled the temple and the country. Carter confirms that situation: "Syria-Palestine was marked by a village-based economy. Agricultural surplus was extracted from the countryside to support both

---

20. Gerstenberger, *Leviticus*, 8.
21. Briant, *From Cyrus*, 810.

the urban elite and the broader Persian infrastructure."[22] People faced an uncomfortable situation. Where to go? How to find shelter?

Cyrus probably never sent a Persian as satrap to govern another people. He was always satisfied with their native princes. However, as Xenofon reminds us: "He did receive tribute from them, and whenever he needed forces, he made a requisition upon them for troops."[23]

Tunnermann points out that, within the Persian politics of domination, the army was an element of extreme importance. Till the beginning of the Greco-Persian wars there was no army that could resist them. The army was divided by "military toparchies" and distributed in garrisons. The toparchies included many satrapies and were commanded by military officials to whom the commanders of the other satrapies were subordinated. Persians constituted most of their contingent and their total number can be estimated at one million. Ten thousand "immortal warriors" constituted the army's spine. They got this name because every time one soldier died, another came to replace him. The first regiment (the first 1,000 soldiers who represented the Persian nobility) constituted the king's personal guard. Representatives of Iranian and Elamite tribes formed the other nine regiments of immortals. During the principal military campaigns, peoples from all the Empire were forced to send a certain number of soldiers.[24]

Tribute Paid in Coins (and the Implications)

It can be noticed that, while the former empires that dominated the region used to accept products from agriculture and flocks as part of tax payment, the Persians demanded the payment in gold or coins. Again, Carter explains: "The Persian period also saw the emergence of coinage and its expanded use within the economy. Several hoards of coins have been discovered throughout Syria-Palestine, indicating both gradual movement toward a moneyed economy and a series of local mints."[25] It is possible to estimate the consequences of this change in a region that lived primarily from agriculture. That is, Judea had to get money to pay

---

22. Carter, *Syria-Palestine*, 408.
23. Briant, *From Cyrus*, 64.
24. Tunnermann, *As reformas*, 23.
25. Carter, *Syria-Palestine*, 408.

the tribute by selling its products. The peasants' necessity of selling their products only increased the exploitation they themselves suffered.

The spread of coins marks a difference between the time of Persian domination and the previous ones. The first coins mentioned in the Old Testament were the golden Persian drachmas (Ezra 2:69; Neh 7:70–72), coined by the Persian Emperor after 517 BCE. The golden drachma weighed about 8.4g, and the Persian silver *shekel* weighed 5.6g. They were exchanged in a proportion of one to twenty, corresponding to the relation of one to thirteen between gold and silver.[26] The king's money had greater value compared to the innumerous local coins, coined in silver. For Tunnermann, "There were three kinds of silver and the King's treasure chamber was aware of that; so, they evaluated the coins only after weighing them. However, the tribute was based on pure silver."[27]

The silver coin from Judea that weighed 2.08g was particularly suitable to pay the mercenaries. According to Herodotus, "Darius would have been the first one to fix the contribution that people had to pay to the Government."[28] The reason for the coinage is linked to the Government's interest in regularizing tributes. Herodotus adds that, "Darius acted like a trader in everything he did."[29]

Judea's inhabitants had no silver mine from which they could obtain the money that was demanded from them. Therefore, they had to get money for the tribute by selling the excess of agricultural products. For that, there was a fixed tribute in silver that each landowner had to pay (Neh 5:4).

To conclude this point, Kippenberg reminds us that the burden of the values demanded by the government was laid totally upon the farmers' shoulders because in Judea there was neither a silver mine nor a considerable production of manufactured products such as the ceramic made in the Atic Pottery. Thereby, the peasants' families, who lived on what their land produced, had to try to specialize in producing what was more profitable. The products usually sold were barley, olive products, and cattle.[30]

26. Kippenberg, *Religião*, 47.
27. Tunnermann, *As reformas*, 25–26.
28. Kippenberg, *Religião*, 48.
29. Ibid., 48.
30. Ibid., 50.

Tribute was a kind of mechanism through which the Persian Empire drained people's life. All peoples who acknowledge Persian supremacy were required to pay tribute in kind or in precious metal to the central authority, not to mention the military contingents of oarsmen that they had to provide in compliance with any royal requisition. However, the Temple in Jerusalem mediated the relation between empire and people. The Temple was responsible for collecting the products from the peasants. At that time, the Temple started being the economic, political, and religious center of the country. As time went by, the High Priests who controlled the Temple became more powerful. Indeed, they were the ones who carried out the political will of Judea's Persian imperial overlords. One part of these agricultural products was retained in the Temple itself, and the other was sold to pay the tribute to the Persians. One conclusion seems to be obvious: this strong necessity of selling the products from the farms in order to get coins to pay the tribute led to agriculture becoming a trade market. As a result, people stopped planting only for their subsistence and started planting for commerce. Therefore, they bore a double taxation: tribute charged by the Persian Empire and tribute charged by the Temple in Jerusalem. Here is Leith on this point:

> From the Persian's standpoint, the Temple in Jerusalem, like temples elsewhere, contributed various forms of tribute to the state—revenues, goods, and services. Persia's Judean proxies in control of the Temple were responsible for raising this tribute from a local population already struggling to pay the tithe and annual levy they owed the Persians (Neh 5). High-priestly families also administered the material and fiscal resources that accrued to the Temple as part of the sacrificial system. Thus, whoever controlled the Jerusalem Temple also participated significantly in the economic activity of the land and enjoyed high social and economic status. As the social elite, the Temple community could dictate the terms by which an outsider could qualify for membership in their group and thereby share its privileges.[31]

Nehemiah and Deprivation in Judea

The story revealed through Job's experience is presumably addressed to the people who owned lands and stocks but had lost their possessions. Their loss was caused by internal (i.e., Judean) and external (i.e.,

---

31. Leith, *Israel*, 298–99.

Persian) factors. It is important to notice that both these channels were instruments of dehumanization. We may even say they were the most penetrating instruments in those people's skin. It is before this alienating scenario that the official theology was born. It was born with the desire to teach peasants, by means of catechesis, to have patience—Job's patience—accept everything and, mainly, be silent. So, the picture we see is very bleak. The official theology was created in an agrarian crisis as the agriculture itself started being directed to the international market and no longer to the peasant's subsistence. The description given by Neh 5:1–5 reveals an extremely sharp social conflict:

> Now there arose a great outcry of the people and of their wives against their Jewish brothers. For there were those who said, "With our sons and our daughters, we are many. So let us get grain, that we may eat and keep alive." There were also those who said, "We are mortgaging our fields, our vineyards, and our houses to get grain because of the famine." And there were those who said, "We have borrowed money for the king's tax on our fields and our vineyards. Now our flesh is as the flesh of our brothers, our children are as their children. Yet we are forcing our sons and our daughters to be slaves, and some of our daughters have already been enslaved, but it is not in our power to help it, for other men have our fields and our vineyards" (ESV)

The common people complained of having to indenture their children to be able to eat; some had to mortgage their fields and vineyards to pay the royal tribute. In order to restore peace, Nehemiah took astonishing measures: he no longer collected the "governor's bread" tax. However, we need to realize that this act had primarily symbolic value (and perhaps some self-justification), even though it takes into account the combined effect of the royal levies and satrapy taxes. The basic problem lies at the level of relations between rich and poor: by lending money at interest, the former starved the latter. It can be said that the impoverishment of the small land-holders was thus not simply an automatic result of the imposition of tribute: tribute only played the role of revealing and accelerating what already existed in the specific context of class relations of Jewish society. The various taxes also converged so that everyone had to pay for maintenance of the Temple and its personnel: a one-third shekel head tax (Neh 10:33), as well as "first-fruits and tithes, . . . those portions . . . awarded . . . to . . . the cantors and gatekeepers too" (Neh 12:44–47).

The burden was so heavy that during Nehemiah's absence, the Jews had stopped bringing "the tithe of corn, wine, and oil to the storehouses" (Neh 13:12). Consequently, we can read the forty chapters that form the core of the Book of Job as an echo of the peasant women's protest in Neh 5:1–5 and notice that Job's wife's speech is presented by the text as a counter-speech. People were required to pay various taxes to the satrap himself. The satrap, who was the image of the king in each province, also had a luxurious life, moving from one residences to another during the year.

However, it is necessary to verify the extent of Nehemiah's work. Consider the words of Briant as he points out that Nehemiah's jurisdiction was:

> The country of Judah (Neh 5:14), that is, the province (*medinah*) that on fourth century coins is called Yehud. Apparently the province, including Jerusalem itself, was divided into districts (*pelek*), which probably were tribal in origin but perhaps also corresponded to fiscal subdivisions. Like the governor of other provinces in the region, Nehemiah acted under the authority of the governor of Trans-Euphrates, who was undoubtedly based in Damascus. This governor, it seems, held an estate within the jurisdiction of the province that was something like a satrap paradise and the inhabitants of the province were required to perform corvee on his estate" (Neh 3:7).[32]

Following the model of a "real" satrap, the governor of Judah received a special tax—called the Satrap's Table—that allowed him to supply his table everyday and to entertain his guests:

> From the day the king appointed me governor in the land of Judah, from the twentieth to thirty-second year of King Artaxerxes I, for twelve years, neither my kinsmen nor I ever ate governor's bread. Now the former governors, my predecessors, had been a burden on the people, from whom they took forty silver shekels each day as their subsistence allowance, while their servants oppressed the people too. But I, fearing God, never did this . . . Jews and officials to the number of a hundred and fifty ate at my table, not to mention those who came to us from the surrounding nations. Everyday, one ox, six fine sheep, and poultry, were prepared at my expenses. Every ten days skins of wine were brought in bulk. But even so, I never claimed the governor's subsistence allowance,

---

32. Briant, *From Cyrus*, 585.

since the people already had burden enough [of the construction work] to bear (Neh 5:14–18).

There is no doubt that the Jewish community was subjected to paying tribute to the kings as well as various taxes, like the satrap's table. However, who were the "former governors" mentioned by Nehemiah? According to Briant, a list of the governors of the province between Zerubbabel and Nehemiah had been reconstructed from a series of seal impressions and bullas found in Judah: "Elnathan (perhaps Zerubbabel's successor), Yezo-ezer (early fifth century), Ahzai (early fifth century)—all of them Jews (as were Zerubabbel and Nehemiah)."[33] Then, with Nehemiah, the Jerusalem community continued enjoying internal autonomy, as it had since Cyrus's time. However, at the same time, it had to exhibit its submission to Achaemenid (Persian) authority, especially in the area of tribute.

One of Nehemiah's main tasks was to levy the royal tribute (Neh 5:3). He also had a military function, since he put Jerusalem in a state of military readiness and entrusted the citadel to one of his close associates. Leith notes that Judah was only one sub-province in the Persian fifth satrapy, which comprised Babylon (until 482), Syria-Palestine (including the coastal Phoenician city-states), and Cyprus.[34] Unlike the Assyrians, the Babylonians had not brought deportees from elsewhere into Palestine. But Palestine was nevertheless the home of peoples who had been displaced and whose national identity had been threatened during the unrest of the sixth century: Philistines, Judaists, Samarians, Moabites, Ammonites, Edomites, Arabs, and Phoenicians.

Briant claims that from the Persian point of view Nehemiah's mission was to establish a new basis for assessing tribute and guaranteeing regular payment, and, moreover, that "his reforms can be compared with those carried out by Artaphernes in 493 in the cities of Ionia that had been ravaged by war and social tension."[35] In a region where Persian control was threatened by international military adventurism, Jerusalem became an inland defensive city and possibly a new center for the collection and storage of imperial revenues (delivered in kind or not in coin before the late fifth century). When Nehemiah lightened the tax burden, rather than aiming at some sort of rapprochement between peasant and aristocracy,

---

33. Ibid., 488.
34. Leith, *Israel*, 286.
35. Briant, *From Cyrus*, 586.

he may have been trying to minimize an increased tax burden, caused by the need to maintain the new garrisons. The implied criticism of the Persian rules by the later author/editor of Ezra-Nehemiah (Ezra 9:8–9, Neh 5:1–19) may reflect Persia's tightened grip on Judah and the economic consequence of Ezra's and Nehemiah's work. Nehemiah helped Judean peasants by suppressing excesses of usury and remitting the taxes paid for his own maintenance. However, he was also willing, as an upper-class member of the influential eastern Diaspora, to exclude the those not considered "pure" Jews—the "people of the land"—from his definition of "Israel."

Besides the exploitation and impoverishment already mentioned, it is important to recall that the social environment where people lived favored the creation of a new theological language. Such language had the objective of justifying their pain and inhuman suffering. Kessler´s analysis is essential to understand this period: "All the elements of indebtedness, impoverishment, and miserablization that already existed in the late period of monarchy can be observed in the Persian period as well. It can also be said that the tendency to miserablization is bigger."[36]

Not only had the social and political situation of the people undergone substantial changes, but also new themes and theological practices began to be introduced as a reference for the people who had been in the Babylonian exile. It was in this new scenario that the belief that wealth was an undoubted signal of God's blessing started to grow stronger. The purest would be the richest and the impure would be the poor and the sick. Previously, the signal of God's blessing was the possession of *land* (Gen 12:1), but now *wealth* was the signal of God's presence and blessing started being identified with wealth.

---

36. Kessler, *História*, 177.

2

Theology and Anti-Theology in the Book of Job

WITH HIS APPARENT REBELLIOUSNESS, Job tries to deal with one of the fundamental issues that most concerned the Israelite wise men: the theology of reward. According to this theology, God gives wealth to some people and poverty to others. In this way, the rich are and go on being rich because they are righteous; the poor are and continue to be poor because they did not trust in God's justice, that is, they are sinners. Because of that, it is not difficult to understand the outcry that comes from Job's lips revealing the terrible state he is in. "That is why I cannot keep quiet: in my anguish of spirit I shall speak, in my bitterness of soul I shall complain" (7:11).

It seems to me that this theology of reward brought about a change in the way that people thought about the place where God can be found. It introduced, I suggest, a theological shift. Let me explain: The exodus tradition shows a divinity with a historical density, that is, a God who *comes down from the heavens* precisely to deal with human suffering: "The Lord said, 'I have indeed seen the misery of my people in Egypt. I have heard them crying out because of their slave drivers, and I am concerned about their suffering. So I have come down to rescue them'" (Exod 3:7–8). For the biblical theology of Exodus, God is *not remote* in heaven *but near* on earth, walking beside the people who suffer. If we turn our eyes to the New Testament, we will come to the same conclusion. The Gospel of John presents us a Christ who incarnates and takes on human history as a true protagonist. In both cases, the best place to find the divinity is not in heaven but in human history—in the midst of the pain and suffering of those who live on the peripheries of the world. In the theology of reward, however, God is located in heaven, watching and rewarding each one according to their righteousness and their obedience to the divine law. This God is not near and does not stand in solidarity with the suffering.

The masters and doctors of religion, shaped by the teaching of the theology of reward, asked the suffering righteous to be *patient*. Their suffering would be *brief* and their faithful patience would finally be *rewarded*. *Extended* suffering, however, could not be innocent suffering. Therefore, from the perspective of this theology, the idea of Job being *both* an honest and righteous man *and* poor and miserable over an increasing period of time is be *inconceivable*. In this way the concrete situation of a man, that is, his prosperity or his disgrace, would be taken as signals of the righteousness or unrighteousness of his actions. The Book of Job challenges precisely this traditional view of suffering. In light of this, the fact of the Book of Job being included in the canon gets more significant; after all, it is a subversive text that presents a critique of the traditional wisdom, the theoretical theology, and the economic arrangements of its time!

Indubitably, in the theology of reward we are presented with a dogma. And we know dogmas are not open for discussion or any kind of protest. However, how can we remain silent with a pain that refuses to leave our body? How can we keep quiet if the soul itself starts crying? The vision of sons and daughters dying or being enslaved does not work as an analgesic, but as a fuel that leads to a protest. A careful reading of Neh 5:1–5 shows us women acting like protagonists. It is principally they who protest and do it vehemently. But, let us note: their attitude is contrary to the theology of reward. The only action suitable for them—according to the theology of reward—would be to remain silent, waiting for God's justice. Protesting against injustice reflected a failure to trust in God's justice; and worse: it was like not accepting God's plan and, therefore, cursing it. Consequently, arising from Job's experience, we discover a new thesis: *not every evil is a punishment for a sin*. The righteous can also live in situations of poverty and suffering. Indeed, Job's experience shows that the righteous' suffering is not an unusual and exceptional reality. After all, isn't it true that human history is interspersed with the outcries of the righteous who are victimized and the innocent who suffer? Isn't it also true that history very often is established as a field dominated by wicked and violent men? The experience of Job proclaims from its very beginning that there is no correlation between sin and suffering, between virtue and reward. That logic is hard for us to break.

The theology of reward can also be seen reflected in the Book of Proverbs (Prov 3:1–12). It shares this traditional presumption that suffering in one's life is punishment for a sin and reward for righteousness is given in this life. However, the quotidian experience asks for a better theology for experienced reality refuses this vision of the human fate. Even good men suffer or die without enjoying any happiness and wicked men succeed, enjoying life with wealth and pleasures. The wise men from the Bible used all their theological knowledge to try to explain why good people suffered and bad ones kept living in pleasure, but what they produced was only a negative perception about God. God in this sense is always the biggest of big brother. He is always waiting for someone to do something wrong to punish. The situation grew so complex that the expression formulated by Epicure and cited by Lactancio, became emblematic: "If God wants to exterminate evil but is not able, he is impotent; if he is able but does not want, he is cruel with mankind; if he neither wants nor is able, he is both impotent and cruel; if he wants and is able, then why does evil exist and is not exterminated?"

But we cannot isolate the biblical musings on suffering. After all, the Oriental vision had already posed the same problem (there are Sumerian and Akkadian versions about the "sufferer righteous man"). However, the solutions presented there were totally unconvincing. In this scenario, where theological answers did not match lived reality, the Book of Job aims to draft a way out: not all evils suffered are a punishment for sin; and the righteous man can also suffer. I presume God wants the good to live peaceful and happy lives; but sometimes, not even God is able to make it come true. The innocent also suffers in this life, facing many things they do not deserve—losing jobs, getting sick, and watching their children suffer. Let us remember Etty Hillesum, a twenty-nine year old Jewish woman who, not long before she died in the gas chambers of Auschwitz, prayed:

> Dear God, these are anxious times. Tonight for the first time I lay in the dark with burning eyes as scene after scene of human suffering passed before me. I shall promise You one thing, God, just one very small thing: I shall never burden my today with cares about my tomorrow, although that takes some practice. Each day is sufficient unto myself. I shall try to help You, God, to stop my strength ebbing away, though I cannot vouch for it in advance. But

one thing is becoming increasingly clear to me: that You cannot help us, that we must help You to help ourselves. And that is all we can manage, these days and also all that really matters: that we safeguard that little piece of You, God, in ourselves, and perhaps in others as well. Alas there doesn't seem to be much You Yourself can do about our circumstances, about our lives. Neither do I hold You responsible. You cannot help us but we must help You and defend Your dwelling place inside us to the last (apud Connor: 1986, 12).

Adversities can happen in our lives, but it does not mean God is punishing us for something we did wrong. Disgrace definitely does not come from God. He is not our adversary or the reason for our tragedies. On the contrary, God is our ally and the very source where we can find strength and capacity to bear the difficulties and to overcome the obstacles, and determination to keep going on towards our objectives.

I could say that life without suffering exists in dreams only, never in reality. It is not atypical for a healthy life to comprise some suffering. However, such situation does not happen as a painful punishment, but as a result of human injustice and as a dark spot in a finite existence that, eventually, causes suffering because there is not another way. It is not possible to exorcize suffering from human history. If we try to do so, we run the risk of stopping being human. Because of that, we should be vigilant with regard to reward theologies that still emerge in the ecclesiastic quotidian.

The message in the Book of Job and the experience it recounts are not easy to understand at first sight. Care is required to understand it as a simplistic reading of the book—applying its message directly to our own different lives and experiences—can lead to some mistakes. From the beginning we need to make a clear distinction between Job's speeches and his friend's speeches for they are very different. It can be said that the Book of Job allows for a double warning that we can summarize as follows:

a. never infer sin from suffering (Job's friends' mistake); and,

b. never infer God's enmity in relation to the sufferer (Job's mistake).

Job's story was already known in Palestine. In Ezek 14:14, we are introduced to a triad of wise men and Job is among them, along with Noah and Daniel. It is important to recall that the Book of Ezekiel was written at least 150 years before the Book of Job. It is quite possible that the story told in the latter was not of Jewish origin, as Job is presented as a foreigner, coming from Hus (1:1). Yet, in light of Ezek 14:14, his story seems to have been proverbial among the Judahites from at least the seventh century BCE.

Job is considered as one of the "Orient's sons." That is to say that there is no effort from the narrator to establish a geographic site for the story. Our protagonist, in the text of the book, has neither had a definite place or time—Job's story (without family names) can be considered the history of each one of us. But what matters for our purposes is that Job was *not an Israelite* and that he belonged to the wise clans. So, Job's story can be considered the history of each one of us. The prologue that introduces the book aims to show the reader that Job, while he is not an Israelite, is a righteous and devout person. His characteristics stand out in the text: "This man was blameless and righteous; he feared God and shunned evil" (1:1).

Great speeches can be found in the Book of Job. In these speeches, Job's friends—Eliphaz, Bildad, and Zophar, plus the conservative and quite cheeky Elihu—argued fiercely around the same thesis: God's righteous man does not suffer; he has no pain; he experiences no trial or oppression. The author's own position on this point is made clear by the preeminence that he gives to Job's speeches. These taken together amount to twenty whole chapters (513 verses), while Eliphaz's speeches account only to four chapters (113 verses), Bildad's three (49 verses), Zophar's two (also 49 verses) and Elihu's six (165 verses).

With their theological construction, Job's friends insist on showing him that if he is facing difficulties and merciless suffering, the cause is his sins. Job, on the other hand, refuses their teasing words by calling them liars, advisors of defeated, and annoying consolers (Job 6:14–17, 27–28). To each speech of their friends, Job gives a convenient answer. In the end, even God abjured the pre-packaged theological speeches of Job's friends. Eliphaz, Bildad, Zophar and Elihu's speeches are full of beautiful words, apparent humility, and great and eloquent statements, all with the unique purpose of defending God. The friends' speeches intend to enclose Job within the theology of reward's vicious circle. We can see four friends, four speeches and variations on the same theology. They offer all the typical solutions. Every stock phrase we have already heard from clergy stereotypes or read in devotional books is here. And, in fact, they are rather intelligent, but the conclusion of the book is that none of these remedies is adequate or even correct. On the contrary, the theological speech formulated by them—or at least reproduced by them—seeks to infect Job with what is, in fact, a theological disease more deadly than the pain he is currently suffering.

The four friends' speeches represent the official theological vision in Israel, that is, they defend God's justice and claim that men's actions and their consequent sins are the cause of any disgrace in human life. The friends talk from an official, centrally-sanctioned perspective while Job talks from the periphery—poverty, mourning, abandonment, infirmity, and humiliation. It is necessary to emphasize that we need to have a great discernment not to move away from the true understanding about God. As Rohr points out "the three and eventually four friends of Job are intent on preserving their notion of God, their notion of Job, and their notion of justice at all costs."[1]

Indeed, their speeches are a set of words that inadvertently forms an anti-theology. The anti-theology looks like theology but it is not theology. One of Mathews' parables illustrates this matter quite well. He talks about two houses (Matt 7:24–27): one is built on rock and the other on sand. They were in all equal and served as a shelter for their inhabitants in the same way. The radical difference was presented when the storm came. So too with the anti-theology of the four "friends" of Job. Their eloquent and beautiful words come from a *distorted* vision of God and of reality. That is why Job represents the theology and his four questioners represent the anti-theology!

What a great number of things are presented as theology nowadays but are only mere theological caricature! Theology is the confession of faith in a God who demands us to have a life transforming and world transforming experience with him. This experience has to be based on clear and safe facts that are able to guide us firmly towards the knowledge of our liberator God. Theology is life and defends life. Anti-theology displaces God from the exact center where he should be and, in one way or another, it converts the man into the start point of the route to understand God. Theology presents what God thinks of the human being while anti-theology presents what the human being thinks of God.

---

1. Rohr, *Job*, 33.

A spiral of discursive violence begins to appear in the words of each friend as Job refuses to take their advice on board. Their words become aggressive; and their attacks virulent and brutal. Although the theological speeches are strongly uttered, Job does not give up. Instead of being quiet, he reacts and refuses the anti-theology his friends present in such beautiful colors.

Again, it is necessary to recall the care we need to take with some theologies that walk along our ecclesiastic roads. Many of them work as anti-theology. They do not talk about God but about an anti-God. It is possible to say that every theology plays some social role in our social organization. There is not any neutral theology, even if we make an effort to build it. Every theology talks from its social place. It seems to me that Job possesses this theological intuition. In response to the well-made and organized speeches of his friends, Job puts himself in their comfortable shoes and says, "I would say the same words if I were in your place" (16:4). Listen to Gutierrez: "The friends talk as they do because they have not experienced the abandonment, poverty, and pain that Job has . . . [T]he dividing line is drawn by personal experience, which sometimes brings a painfully acquired closeness to God, which these untouched theologians with their arguments do not know."[2]

As they speak theologically, from their comfortable and safe place, Job's friends are only able to glimpse the periphery of Job's world. Their words show sympathy. With the movement of their lips, they try to console their friend. But what they say is worth nothing. On the contrary, their words are an anti-theology that only increases the pain of the one who listens them. And, consequently, Job rejects a way of theologizing that does not take account of concrete situations or the sufferings and hopes of human beings and forgets the gratuitous love and unbounded compassion of God.

For me, Job gives them a true theology lesson, that is, he shows his friends that, in the face of the injustice and exploitation that ruins life, the theologians are invited to rethink their theology from these social conditions. Contact with the defeated people who live on the periphery of the world forces the theologian to inquire himself about the tools he is using to do his theological labor. Possibly, some questions would arise from Job's experience as we listen to the theological proposal of his friends.

2. Gutierrez, *Falar*, 30.

These questions reveal the true character and sense of theology. The example of some of these questions shows that there is neither theological communication nor theological practice without context. It means that the ways to elaborate theology are by way of answers to questions that have arisen from the interaction of people with the environment where they live. Questions such as:

- What is the application of theology?
- What is its message?
- Who is the subject that is behind its elaboration?
- Which interests does it defend?

These are only some of the relevant questions and if we do not ask them we run the risk of taking the path of anti-theology. After all, in Job's experience, God and pain are not contradictory! Therefore, it would be useless to observe Job's experience, as if it were a fictional eschatology that alienates people from their own. That is to say that we should not see the present situation through the lens of failure, poverty, and sickness or even demolish the present to build utopia. Instead, we should observe his experience, as it was a theology of human history; Job remains in history and seeks, insistently, not the mere cathartic elimination of pain and poverty, but fundamentally, their theological interpretation. Job always speaks from his reality. He does not try to alienate himself but instead tests the theology of his "friends" to see if it connects with day-to-day reality. Maybe one of the main lessons that Job teaches us is warning against relying too much on words: they are not so naive or neutral, let alone the theological words.

It can be said that the principal function of the friends' speeches is to restate a traditional understanding of the nature of God. One understanding might have been held by many, if not most of the first readers of the book and taken for granted as a fundamental principle on which their lives had always been based and on which they had thought that they could rely: that God is a just God who is concerned with the lives of ordinary individual human beings and who always rewards the righteous and punishes the wicked. So, according to Whybray, "the readers would recognize in the speeches of the friends the expression of this familiar and fundamental doctrine. These speeches, then, were intended to be taken seriously by the readers as statements of what they had always believed."[3]

The core of the Book of Job, written in poetry, demonstrates a new theology. In it the theme "patience" is not found. Instead, we can see the theme of a *rebel* Job. The analysis of his daily life allows us to claim that Job is a denial of the official dogmas sustained by his friends. We can even say that we are before a representation of a crisis within official theology. The author of the Book of Job used the temporary misfortune of the hero as a scenario for his poem in which conventional wisdom is questioned. The principal problem of the book is presented in the following way: Job, the righteous, suffers indescribable pains for which neither he nor his friends have enough explanation.

It is quite common to hear that in the Book of Job the main character is the symbol of patience. That is not true! The fact is that a tradition that shows Job as the symbol of patience was created. Actually, Job did not yield himself to temptation, suffering, and the dangerous insinuations of his friends and relatives. He cannot be seen as a passive person at all. On the contrary, he argued with everyone, including God, whom he even challenged (10:1–22). Job was restless and an inquirer. His attitude, to his friends, seemed a true blasphemy. Job's interpretation during the centuries was based on a mistake. As the personification of patience, resignation and perseverance, he was reduced to a bizarre promise of solace after the trial. The well-known phrase "the patience of Job" comes from the New Testament, not from the Old Testament. The Epistle of James (5:11) points to the *hypomene* of Job as an example to the community. The word was rendered "patience" in most of the Bible, but modern translations usually and correctly render it as "steadfastness". That is exact; Job is steadfast, not patient. However, we cannot deny that we are before one of the most extraordinary and outstanding testimonies of faith in the Old Testament.

The author of the Book of Job takes Job's suffering as a prototype of the suffering faced by the people of God. Suffering is an occasion which opens the door for drama, but the most intense theme is the justice of God. The friends defend the wise traditional theology that wants to defend God at the expense of a human being, even if the human being is shattered and suffering unfairly. The friend's arguments are based on

---

3. Whybray, *Job*, 17.

tradition; they accuse in order to defend their theology but do not progress on their discussion. Job, however, reflects from his own reality and because of that, his speech presents innovative characteristics. Would the God presented by his friends be the true God? During the course of the book, we realize that in the friend's speeches there is no allusion to the reality lived by Job, not even to the question of justice Job had posed. Maybe this fact is the confirmation (as well as many other parts of the book are), that the friends' speeches represent the theology of order and submission to a providential destiny that regulates the cosmos, but they do not face the injustice suffered by human beings. So, the friend's speeches are the typical speeches of certain consoling practices!

Job is sick; wounds cover his skin; ashes are aplenty to express his mourning or even to accompany his prayers to God. He who was once eminent within his city is now outside it, in the position of an excluded person (Job 2:7-8, 12-13). Maybe he was mistaken for a leper because lepers were forced to live outside the cities to take away their infirmities from the others. They were also considered people punished by God and, therefore, unworthy to take part in the life of the city. As a diseased person, Job's place, at that moment, is the periphery of life.

Nevertheless, Job demonstrates "steadfastness" till the end. His condition is deeply sad and makes those who watch him sad. Our protagonist leaves home to live outside his village. His new place is now a pile of ash, garbage and excrement where sick people wait for death. His journey from "home" to the pile of garbage represents the way of anti-life. In such a way Satan wants from Job a *declared* blasphemy—of the kind that Job was afraid his children might utter on the days of celebration (1:5)—not a mere interior blasphemy. In his path of exclusion Job is completely lonely!

We can say that Job's crisis expresses the many and varied crises that people face today. In this sense, the Book of Job gets a special value as it becomes a mirror that reflects our own ordinary experience. The dominant pastoral orientation given by Job's friends from his experience should be contested in order to discuss the problem of the righteous who suffers. So, it can be said that the author of the text presents the traditional solace of Job's friends in order to show its inadequacy.

For a while, Job accepted the afflictions that God had put upon him without complaint. In his first speech, however, we start noticing another Job and this time we hear from his lips a sound of protest.

All of us have the right to question God. Jesus himself did it: "My God, my God, why have you forsaken me?" (Matt 27:46). Job's friends did not want him to ask questions (4:17–21). But Job would not accept a theology that denies questioning just because everything has been previously ordained. Job does not let his voice be silenced by the strength of official theological speech (7:11). Therefore, he convincingly says that he would continue questioning: "Be quiet because I am going to speak, no matter what happens" (13:13). The mistake is not asking questions, but the desire of asking questions whose answers had already been given even before the questions had been asked. So, the mistake is in giving answers simply based on logic or on human convenience, as Job's friends did.

The trial Job is facing is so devastating that it will end up in an outcry that is a metaphor for human affliction and suffering. Through his outcry, Job is expressing his solidarity with all humanity. His trial does not isolate him, but brings him closer to us. "We no longer can bear it," is the despairing outcry that comes from the throat of each one of us. Job wishes death more than life. His question "Why?" still echoes in our own lips.

THE THEOLOGY OF A TRADER GOD—ELIPHAZ

Job's friends remind him of the just order of this world governed by God, and suggest it would be convenient for him to examine his own life. Using his utilitarian moral, Eliphaz presents and represents the official theology of reward. He insistently affirms the dogma of rewarding justice. For him, people harvest misery and injustice because they have sown and cultivated them. Consequently, they perish and are consumed by God's breath. In his speech it is possible to see that the principle of the theology of reward is so absolute and universal that it is applied even to animals. "At the breath of God they are destroyed; at the blast of his anger they perish. The lions may roar and growl; yet the teeth of the great lions are broken. The lion perishes for lack of prey, and the cubs of the lioness are scattered" (4:9–11). There is no way to escape. What Eliphaz announces as is merely what he previously thought and was already part of his theology. To sum up, Eliphaz is concerned about what human beings think about God, instead of what God thinks about human beings. He is especially concerned with a particular human being, Job, called to be a faithful witness in a situation of trials and temptations.

Elipahz gives his interpretation about Job's suffering, as if it was a correction. For him, Job suffers not because of his enemies (as in most of the plea Psalms), but as a consequence of some sin he is not able to identify (Job 5:18–20). In this sense, Yahweh's punishment is a signal of his love and the one who receives it is fortunate. Consequently, he thinks Job has no reason to lose his desire for life or to curse his birth. Eliphaz's theology is expressed with the intent on convincing Job about his culpability. Therefore, Eliphaz does not hesitate in affirming that God is able to hurt.

In Eliphaz's speeches there is a nullification of the victimizing strength of those who hold the power—political or economic—and yet there is an emptiness in his generalizing comments about "enemies." In Job's speech, on the other hand, the enemies can and must be specified, just like the prophets do when they nominate them as military and political leaders, kings, king's sons, queen, tax collectors, usurers, noble ladies, nobles, priests, false prophets, landholders, judges, and king's ministers. The violent acts are specifically inflicted upon the poor (24:2–4) threatening, therefore, their existence. A possible question might enhance our reflection: Is the human beings' temporariness something undeniable and irrefutable? If so, why are many of them sentenced to die prematurely? The answer to this question would possibly insert us into the area of missionary responsibility or into the area of a theology that makes itself missionary.

On behalf of religion, Eliphaz sets aside Job's *concrete suffering* to dedicate his theological speech to *a doctrinal theme*. But we should ask: which comes first, religion or life? When religion lets life be set up in a second plane it starts defending a situation that produces death. Subsequently, Eliphaz and his friends were caught up in this trap. Eliphaz's argument is clear: The wicked person suffers because of his wickedness. The friends' theological speeches seek to refuse Job's statements that God treats equally both the wicked and the innocent. Unlike Job, Eliphaz does not make use of *his own experience* but of the tradition that bears with it the authority of several generations of wise men. To defend the established ideological order, Eliphaz is ready to direct Job's case without even investigating it. He represents Job as a wicked, rebel, and impious man. Eliphaz sees the world in a mirror that distorts reality. And, possibly, his reality is distorted because the distortion caused by the inner chaos has already been established. Eliphaz tries to force Job to accept a quite traditional doctrine. He clearly shows no concern about the situation of extreme suffering his friend is facing and avoids being questioned by it as well. It is amazing to see that neither he nor the other three friends say a single word about Job's affliction. Their concern about defending the doctrine can stifle any kind of compassion. He cannot understand that theology is the second act while life is the first. Theology flows from the life soil and exists to defend life, in particular the life of the poorer ones. To be reliable, every theological action must necessarily be preceded by a reflection and analysis of the concrete human being and his concrete life. If there is a lack of reflection, one runs the risk of adopting theological methods that reduce the human being to an object.

We might say that Eliphaz's theological method is to offer his ideas as having been mediated from the divine realm to him via a "night-vision" (4:12–21). Eliphaz's pretension of presenting himself as a prophet by claiming the right of a special variety of divine revelation does not sustain itself. Nothing is farther from being prophetic, for the truly prophetic reads history as a key source when constructing theological speech. Pseudo-revelations are not the best way to make theology.

Eliphaz presents a god of an extremely alienating religion that blesses all the ones who do not inquire about the actions of religion. Here we see theology of reward as a witness of a mercantile religion. This vision transforms God into a merchant and within a mercantile spirituality, gold never lose its value.

THEOLOGY AS ASSEMBLY LINE: THINKING IS FORBIDDEN—BILDAD

Job's friends' theology does not live on revelation alone! It also draws on a tradition that forbids thinking. Totalitarianism does not present itself with political colors only; We can also speak about a totalitarianism that leads us to create theological systems that twist around themselves and, consequently, establish fundamentalism as the very basic premise for their construction.

According to Rossi, Bildad's theological speech reveals three key things: (a) The unquestionable belief of the tradition that he represented that the punishment of the wicked and the protection of the righteous were a divine law firm and safe—as inviolable, we might say, as the law of cause and effect in Physics; (b) The assumption that these ancestral traditions are untouchable; (c) The fact that Bildad did not think for himself but simply started repeating what he had learned from the ancestral tradition, like a parrot.[4] A possible conclusion is expected: for Bildad the dogma of retribution could not be denied by humans or even by God.

Bildad enters the discussion a bit more exacerbated than Eliphaz. Job continues the discussion without losing his wind, in spite of his weakness: "How long will you say such things? Your words are a blustering wind" (8:2). Now Bildad claims that Job is suffering because he and his children had sinned: "When your children sinned against Him, He gave them over to the penalty of their sin" (8:4). Bildad asserts that Job has only one solution for all his suffering: praying to God and asking for forgiveness and mercy for his sins by showing through his acts that he has really repented: "if you are pure and upright, even now He will rouse himself on your behalf and restore you to your rightful place" (8:6). He assures Job that he, Job, would reach all the success he had before and even more: "Your beginnings will seem humble, so prosperous will your future be" (8:7). However, in this point we can perceive a great irony. Notice that prosperity is ironically not what Job is asking for, but it is fundamental in the world in which Bildad and his friends were caught.

Bildad keeps repeating the same argument, saying that the upright does not suffer. "Can papyrus grow tall where there is no marsh? Can reeds thrive without water? Such is the destiny of all who forget God / so perishes the hope of the godless" (8:11–13). Baldad feels so bothered that he starts attributing the cause of the death of Job's children to his sins. Job should beg for God's help instead of arguing with Him, he says. However, it seems to me that the prophet Ezekiel had already solved this problem with his insights on the responsibility of individuals for their fate (Ezek 18:1–9).

Liverani argues that in the ancient Near East, and particularly in Israel, collective responsibility had two areas of application: a horizontal and a vertical one.[5] The *horizontal collective responsibility* considers responsible for a crime not only the individual authors of the crime, but also their families and the local communities (villages, towns). Thus, when the responsible person was not identified, the community to which he belonged (which evidently had protected him) should assume the burden of guilt. For example "If the merchants of the king of Ugarit are killed

---

4. Rossi, *A falsa*, 58–59.
5. Liverani, *Para além*, 259–60.

in the land of Karkemish . . . and there their killers are not arrested, the Karkemish´s sons shall go to Ugarit and swear: 'We do not know who the murderers are, and the merchants´ goods are gone." This same process of responsibility still echoes in the Deuteronomic legislation: "If someone is found slain, lying in a field in the land the LORD your God is giving you to possess, and it is not known who the killer was, your elders and judges shall go out and measure the distance from the body to the neighboring towns. Then the elders of the town nearest the body shall take a heifer that has never been worked and has never worn a yoke" (Deut 21:1–3). This horizontal responsibility interlaces with the *vertical, generational responsibility*. According to it, children are responsible for their parents' sins "until the seventh generation." There is an obvious connection between this generational responsibility and the rules for inheritance of property: firstly in an automatic way (favoring the eldest son), then with the choice (the various patriarchal blessings on his deathbed), but always from father to son. By taking advantage of the estate assets, the son also assumed the burden of any outstanding issues, not only financial, but also criminal.

Both forms of corporate responsibility entered a crisis gradually through long-term socioeconomic changes, but the national disaster and exile accelerate the crisis. The individual was no longer embedded in a political structure and in a social fabric that protected him and from which he drew sustenance through a regular transfer of ownership. This situation resulted in the formulation of a framework of personal reference in which the individual assumed all his liabilities, but did not intend to assume the others' (as the enlightening writings of Jeremiah and Ezek 31:29–30; 14:13–16).

Notice then the terrifying language of this "theologian" who, to defend his "doctrine," blames a poor father for the death of his beloved sons and daughters. Bildad has no interest in investigating the details of Job's case. At first, Bildad is not inclined to question the justice of God. It is obvious that Job did not accept the appeal to tradition because the tradition did not explain anything; on the contrary, it just complicated things. To follow Bildad's traditional solution, Job should try to forget his affliction, change his expression, and make a cheerful face: "If I say, I will forget my complaint, I will change my expression and smile" (9:27). But Job would not do that at all. For him it would be hypocrisy and a lie. Job was convinced that such behavior would not change the way God was treating him (9:28b). So when Bildad appeals to tradition, he is offering a false conformism to Job.

Actually, Bildad's theological construction is more than simply weird; it is a dangerous theology since it effects the exclusion of human beings. It is not a theology that looks for paths of solidarity. Rather, it reduces the human being to the condition of a worm—"If even the moon is not bright and the stars are not pure in His eyes, how much less man, who is but a maggot, a son of man, who is only a worm" (25:5–6). Such theology breaks the ties of solidarity and points to a society that does not have place for all the people. When Bildad dehumanizes the human being he is legitimizing a theology that produces anti-life, a theology that excludes!

Nevertheless, for a lot of people it is easier to look inside the human being, as if he were a worm. In this way and because of this point of view, it would be possible and even natural to turn away our eyes, our steps, and our hands from the one who suffers or is victimized by hegemonic social, economic, political, and religious forces that undermine the day to day reality.

What is the use of a religion that does not protect the human being? What is the purpose of a theology that does not speak the language of the victim? What is the function of a faith system that does not lead people to meet each other, mainly to meet the one who suffers?

Indeed, Bildad represents the mainstream religion and its (in)consequent theology, which has lost its reference and mission in the world since it has denied life as the first act, thereby undermining authentic theology. In a cosmic vision in which the right to life is more important than the right to possession, the outcry of the poor requires an answer, not as an additional or legal act of generosity but as a demand of justice itself. Bildad is convinced about his theology. This man thinks that he already has the whole truth and he thus behaves in the way most immature religious people tend to: "I know the truth, don't confuse me with the facts." Many of us live that way. We get our "truth" early in life and do not want to be bothered with further evidence.

His words are sharp: "If your sons sinned against Him, they have paid for their sins." We can say that he meant: "Your kids are already dead. Shouldn't you realize you did something wrong?" These are words without mercy. But there is a great irony here. Let us read some verses: "Without delay he will restore his favor to you . . . Your former state will seem to you as nothing beside your new prosperity" (8:6–7).

When we do something wrong, we are punished. This is the alleged teaching. Bildad expounds a version of a natural law: "without water, can the rushes grow?" Just as certain as those natural laws, when a man sins, he is punished, when he is good he is rewarded. It makes sense and it is what many theologies say about God. However, these are not the natural laws that govern our relationship with God.

Baldad can be considered a dogmatist par excellence, and who knows, we might today stereotype him as a "fundamentalist." He refuses to rethink the tradition. He is a professor devoid of charisma!

THEOLOGY AS DEFENSE OF PRIVILEGES—ZOPHAR

As Zophar enters the scene, we come across a theological construction where religion protects the privileged. At first sight, it seems to be an excellent thing. Who wants wisdom? The fact is that only a few men had this wisdom and they kept it in secret. And since it belonged to them only, they wanted ordinary men keep away and stay unaware of it. Living in ignorance, their dependence on the wise men would increase more and more as well the fame of the latter ones. However, here we are before a kind of theology that does not liberate. In fact, it traps us.

The lack of knowledge is the instrument for manipulation. Theology is used to deny dialogue and, therefore, to deny the chance of men gathering together for the common task of interpreting, constructing, and reconstructing their world with creativity. Freire, helps us to understand this relation through a set of questions:

> How can I dialogue if I alienate the ignorant, that is, if I always see it [i.e., ignorance] in the other, never in me? How can I dialogue if I see myself as a different man, virtuous by inheritance, before the others, simple "things" in whom I do not recognize an other like "myself"? How can I dialogue If I feel myself taking part of a ghetto of pure men, owners of the truth and knowledge, for whom all the others who are outside are "those people"? How can I dialogue if I consider that the pronunciation of this world is a task for selected men and that the presence of the masses in history is a signal of deterioration that I should avoid? How can I dialogue if I deny the contribution of others, which I never recognize and by which even I get outraged?[6]

---

6. Freire, *Pedagogia*, 80.

Freire pictures a reality where the absence of dialogue is in force. However, it is important to emphasize that, without dialogue theology does not exist and self-sufficiency is not compatible with the theological dialogue. In a situation where both reality and society are assumed as "given" and as sacred, their order cannot be changed or even questioned. For the one who represents the defeated—as Job does—transgressing the reference mark of this society offers a true challenge, because such a transgression of pre-established values implies a radical reformulation of his way of situating himself in the world.

We frequently subject ourselves, or even subject the faithful, to a type of theological discourse based on the "I will think for you" of the powerful. In the book *1984*, George Orwell interprets this reality very well. In the story the state controlled the thinking of citizens by manipulating the language, among many other means. Experts from the Ministry of Truth created "Newspeak," a language still under construction. After being completed it would prevent the expression of any opinion contrary to the regime. One of the most curious words of Newspeak is the word "doublethink," which corresponds to a concept whereby the individual can cope simultaneously with two diametrically opposed beliefs and accept both.

The purpose of introducing the new language was to reduce the vocabulary the most, in order to reduce people's ability of thinking, making them vulnerable to the party. The elimination of synonyms and the fusion of words made it impossible to relativize. The new words that were created were intended to make many others obsolete. Each edition of the Newspeak dictionary presented less and less vocabulary. Thus, doublethink became easier to be absorbed as people became easier to be controlled

Actually, Zophar's discourse expresses the pathological character of his theology, which dehumanizes the ones who live on the periphery of the world. On one side is Zophar, as the representative of those who know everything, teach everything, interpret everything; on the other side are those who live on the periphery—represented by Job—who know nothing, produce nothing, and receive only the knowledge the others want them to receive. Nevertheless, such pathology denies the ontological vocation each human being has; it denies the man the right of being a participant, not only a mere observer of history. This is a pathological theology that talks about freedom but aims to suffocate the speech that comes from living on the periphery.

Despite everything, if Job were inclined to take part in this highly privileged religious group, his sufferings would cease, according to Zophar: "Oh, how I wish that God would speak, that He would open His lips against you and disclose to you the secrets of wisdom, for true wisdom has two sides. Know this: God has even forgotten some of your sins" (11:6). But Job refuses his proposal and uses irony to answer him: "Doubtless, you are the people, and wisdom will die with you" (12:1).

Zophar does not look carefully at the concept of justice, a theme frequently used by the prophets in Israel in their sermons. In the prophets' theological speech, the destiny of the poor is the key for the justice of a society. Even the laws regarding land and harvest are elaborated to protect the poor (Lev 25; Deut 23:24ff.). Typically, in the Old Testament, the poor are the orphans, the widows, and the foreigners. In this sense, we can understand that their natural enemies are the powerful men, moved by greed. Yahweh demonstrates His justice when He defends the poor from the greed of the powerful (Ps 82:94).

In the Israelites' worldview, it is possible to see a potential and very dangerous enmity of the rich in relation to the poor. In this situation of conflict, Yahweh sides with the poor (Deut 10:16–19). Not by chance, Job uses the concept of *gô'ēl*—"I know that my defender (*gô'ēl*) lives, and that in the end he will stand upon the earth" (19:25). That is, Job claims about the one who defends justice and demands the right of the oppressed (Prov 23:10–11). But what is the meaning of *gô'ēl* / redeemer? The term *gô'ēl* is used in the Hebrew Bible, mainly within the legal material. According to the Holiness Code (Lev 17–26), the land should be perpetually distributed among the families in Israel. But if a man in Israel had debts that he could not pay and his land was taken as a payment for his debts, then his closer kin would become a *gô'ēl* / redeemer, with the responsibility to redeem the land, paying for it so that it would not get into strange hands and be lost to the family forever (Lev 25:23–28).

In the book of Ruth we can see this law being applied when Boaz redeemed the debt of his kinsman Elimelech who had died. From this legal context, the word *gô'ēl* passes to the language of prayer with a meaning of redemption: the liberation the petitioner expects from God's intervention against his enemy (Pss 69:18; 78:35). Respect for the redeemer is applied to Yahweh many times for his feat of freeing Israel from the Egyptian bondage. In Second Isaiah the redemptive epithet is often applied to Yahweh (Isa 43:14; 44:6; 47:4). *Gô'ēl*, thereafter, becomes the defender of justice, the one who claims the right of the oppressed (Prov 23:10–11).

The use of these words by Job seems to indicate that he was possibly representative of the group of peasants who practiced the *gô'ēl* custom. They tried to help each other communally, but this style of life was losing its strength while injustice was increasing. Poverty was growing and they could not keep these practices and expect to be saved from misery by them.

The frequent use of title Redeemer to address God in the Psalms as well as in Second Isaiah might lead us think that in Job it also refers to God. But no! The context excludes God. In that same speech, in verse 11, Job affirms that God is his enemy. Thus, the expression is part of the series of texts in which Job speaks of his heavenly Mediator. Job had previously affirmed his confidence in the existence of a witness in the heavenly court that would act as his interpreter. This character is Job's guardian and in our text he calls him "redeemer" / *gô'ēl*. In Job 5:1 Eliphaz had denied the existence of such a character, but now, before the abandonment of his friends, he is sure that this redeemer really exists.

THE THEOLOGY DEAFNESS—ELIHU

The theology presented by Elihu does not protect human beings either. Instead, it damages them. According to Elihu, God sends him nocturnal revelations in dreams to make him feel mortal. For him, God uses physical suffering to correct human beings, who forget their finitude or their limits. The strong expression Elihu wants to put in Job's lips—"I sinned and perverted what was right" (33:27)—shows us his aged theology. The connection between sickness and sin allows the kind of teaching Elihu wants to communicate; a teaching that Job had exhaustingly heard from his other three "friends".

The only solution for Job would be confessing his sins and repenting from them. This is the conventional advice of religious tradition that always establishes God justice and human injustice when these conflicts happen. As the others, Elihu is not interested in investigating Job's past. For him, it is clear that Job is identified as an impure and rebellious man who despises God's government; as someone dangerous who has to be excluded from their friendship circle, someone who sows doubts and multiplies complaints. For Elihu and his friends, official theology does not tolerate critical questioning. It has no space for doubts as it presents itself as absolute and perfect. So, Elihu claims that the good theology is one that people follow without questioning. Therefore, the verdict of those wise men could not be different: Job has no knowledge to speak (33:5), while Elihu is proud of saying words that express knowledge: "My words come from an upright heart; my lips sincerely speak what I know" (33:3). Eliphaz himself insinuated that Job answered using "empty doctrines" (15:2). Actually, Job—through his experience—sowed doubts among the wise men who thought they were safe about the solidity of their theology. Job is shaking the certainties of the theologians in the established system. They do not allow themselves to be questioned by the challenges of life. Indeed, they do not care about life if they can be illuminated by a theology that sustains their indifference before the ones who suffer. Nevertheless, no theology can make us indifferent before men and women who suffer, under the risk of becoming an anti-theology.

Elihu has no scruples when he affirms that the oppressed will not be heard because they do not address their outcries to the God that has created them. It is a cynical theology that manifests a great disregard for the human being, starting with Job. While considered unreasonable, Job represents all people who are disqualified and devalued by a theology that instead of freeing human beings imprisons them. Elihu's theological argument is insistent: pain is sent by God to call the sinner's attention so that he can repent and enjoy consequent well-being. Its application in Job's case is obvious: Job became a recalcitrant sinner when he refused the warning God sent in order to save him from his bad behavior. Elihu does not accept Job's experience as contrary evidence. If God, as supreme authority, does the good and punishes, that is because there is a reason for that. If God sends affliction to people, it is because he wants to show they are wrong; he wants the sinners to convert from their iniquities.

From the top of his safe place, Elihu allows himself to tell Job that his affliction is a warning coming from the benevolence of God, who is very generous in his Pedagogy. While the other three friends claimed that Job's suffering was only a punishment for his sins, Elihu insists in showing and defending the corrective and educative character of affliction. His suffering had a pedagogical character!

The three other friends claimed that God sent suffering to the wicked—sickness and oppression—as a signal of their injustice. Elihu, on the contrary, says that God uses the suffering pedagogy even for the upright. God is the one who makes the righteous to suffer. But, one question must be intriguing the modern readers: Who has interest in this kind of theology? The answer could not be different: it interests political, religious, and economical groups and others who want before them people who are mild, honest, well-behaved, respectful, polite, submissive to all and everyone without rebelling against injustice and without demanding for their own rights. The problem with this vision is that it neither helps those suffering nor explains their pain. It is primarily concerned with defending God by using words and ideas that turn evil into good and pain into privilege. It is an empty theology which the "friends" believe in more than they believed in their own God.

The theology of reward has assumed a specific form in the Book of Job and will retain that shape throughout the course of the book. In it a life of faith is becomes akin to a commercial relationship between a God-the-businessman and a customer—if you do x, then God will do y.

On one side of the coin, we have the cold handwriting of a doctrine; on the other, the lived experience of pain, calamity, and defeat. From his experience, Job wants to emphasize that his friends have no reason to speak like that because, unlike him, they are not facing the difficult experience of suffering. His outcry is from physical, mental, and moral pain; he suffers in agony so, against a theology of reward he has a single argument: *his personal experience and his observance of history*, in which injustice remains unpunished. His observation and intuition are right: There are only men situated in time and space living in a certain time and in a precise social, cultural, and economical context. Consequently, to be reliable and efficient a theology should take into account man's ontological vocation—the vocation to be a subject—and his life conditions. More than that, with his theology Job tries to show that, to be reliable, a discourse about God should help the human being become a subject.

Job is not the insensitive man, unable to understand as his "friends" declare. Hurt and bothered because Job challenged their concept of theology and religion, from consolers, Job's friends turn into discontent theologians, each one ruder than his predecessor. A brief summary about their speeches is necessary:

a. Eliphaz suggests Job is a sinner;
b. Bildad clearly says Job's children died as a consequence of his sins;
c. Zophar wants to prove to Job his suffering is less than he deserves;
d. Elihu claims that suffering has a pedagogical character.

They perfectly represent the most common masquerades for true biblical faith: ideology, orthodoxy, and conventional heroism.

THEOLOGY IN DEFENSE OF LIFE

It seems to me that our world does not offer space to reflect about poverty, suffering, and human finiteness, as if our culture could not tolerate sad, poor, and defeated people. Nobody wants to experiment with sadness or to analyze what he or she have may done to reach such a state of disillusion. One of the reasons for this situation might be the great problem we have before us: we do not know how to reconcile what is conditional with what is definitive. We live as if we were eternal in a provisory world. Nothing is more unrealistic than this. With no exception, we are absolutely provisory and, consequently, our society ends up making a display of suffering. We need to observe that suffering and poverty are a historical and social construction. If we deny poverty and suffering, we run the risk of denying history and the very society where we live.

Job demonstrates all his vulnerability. He is human, so he suffers. His body is not made of bronze and his strength is not like the stone's. He is not made of steel to keep supporting his suffering. He is completely disappointed at being abandoned by his friends because their theology prevents their pastoral and solidarity action. So, he displays all his weakness in his pain, which does not leave him day or night. Perhaps this is precisely what bothers many theologies—a fear of our own frailty. We are bothered by his speech, which reveals our own weakness in a society that encourages the elevation of victors.

The theological speech of their friends is full of excommunicating feelings. When they look at Job, it is not a feeling of solidarity and compassion that emerges but the feeling of fear and a desire of excommunication. It may not be difficult for them: seeing that Job is sick, they think he is wicked and that God himself had already excommunicated him. It is also very comfortable as there is nothing to be done in this case; it is "the other" who must change his behavior. While Job's experience calls us to be included in it, the friends' speeches seek another path. Their words do not reach the core of the problem, that is, the core of Job's pain. It has nothing to do with mere incomprehension. In fact, they want to remain peacefully in their faith, their God and their theology. They only need to save their traditional conceptions, or rather, the mental horizon they got used to living in.

We can say that the theology of Job's friends is a hostage to its own fear. It is a theology that is not able to break its dogmatic limits and walk towards those who suffer. But, what is the purpose of a theology if it does not reach out its compassionate arms to human beings? It is an anti-theology that makes the emergence of a guilty conscience in Job a possibility, creating an enormous existential confusion in him. In such anti-theology, God was transformed into someone so obsessed by sins that He has as His principal task to hunt man as if they were lions. However, nothing justifies a human being to lack the necessities to live with dignity and to have most of his elementary rights disrespected. Anti-theology, however, not only wants the human being to enter a dehumanization process, but also to live with a profound guilty conscience. In Gutierrez's words: "The suffering and its destructive effect on individuals go far beyond what is seen in a first contact with the world of poor. In such a situation, what content can be assigned to the 'Abba, Father!' that the Spirit cries within us? How are we to proclaim the reign of love and justice to those who live in an inexplicable situation that denies this reign? How are we to bring joyous conviction to our utterance of the name of God?"[7]

Job expresses his indignation. His friends ask him to yield himself to God without even questioning their explanations of his suffering. Their theology would pour contempt on his integrity. But is it possible to have living faith without asking questions? As for his speeches, Job says: That's enough! His friends protected themselves from an attitude of solidarity by elaborating false and alienating speeches. What is the value of a beautiful speech if it does not come with a practice of solidarity? However, in order to defend the official theology, his friends decided to find any situation of sin in Job's life.

---

7. Gutierrez, *Falar*, 13.

The more Job reflects on his experience, the more he accelerates the steps that move him farther from the empty theology of his friends. In doing so, Job realizes that poverty and suffering are bigger than himself. For Job, this poverty and suffering are not fated, but are caused by the wicked, who nonetheless live serene and satisfied lives. These are the same ones who tell the Lord "go away." The wicked are God's rejecters and the enemies of the poor. Probably because of that, the author of the book put into Job's mouth the most radical and cruel description of the wretchedness of the poor that is to be found in the Bible and also to have Job utter a harsh indictment of the powerful who rob and oppress the poor (Job 24:2-17).

The god described by the friends does not correspond to the God that Job discovers more and more and to whom he gets more and more connected. Job's friends were so worried about defending the basic thesis of traditional theology of reward that they did not pay attention to the particularities of Job's experience. Their concern about defending their own interests kept them from allowing themselves to be questioned by Job's experience. In spite of that, Job turns the tables on them: Instead of appealing to the testimony of the ancient wise men, as his friends did, he brings to the discussion, as an evidence, the travelers' experience: "Have you never questioned those who travel? Have you paid no regard to their accounts that the evil man is spared from the day of calamity that he is delivered from the day of wrath? Who denounces his conduct to his face? Who repays him for what he has done? He is carried to the grave, and watch is kept over his tomb" (21:29-32). The travellers' experience testifies that evil people sometimes succeed and are buried with great pomp. Contrary to the theology disseminated by the friends, evil men have long and prosperous lives and are surrounded by their children's activities and die without afflictions.

The description of the wicked's destiny proposed by Job clearly contradicts his friends' description. According to Bildad, the wicked "has no offspring or descendants among his people, no survivor where once he lived" (18:19), but Job presents another vision: "They see their children established around them, their offspring before their eyes" (21:8). Zophar had said that the joy of the wicked is brief and that he would be banished (20:4-9). Bildad adds that infirmity will consume the wicked till death devours his limbs (18:12-14). Job, instead, argues that the wicked's life and death happen in a different way: "They spend their years in prosperity and go down to the grave in peace" (21:13). Eliphaz and Bildad speak about the precarious conditions of the wicked's housing (28:30; 18:15), while Job sees the opposite: "Their homes are safe and free from fear; the rod of God is not upon them" (21:9).

Job's daring consists of applying to the wicked the happiness described of the righteous. He refuses the way of elaborating a theology that has no intrinsic relation to concrete situations, to the suffering and hopes of human beings. He refuses a theology that forgets God's free love and unlimited compassion. Before the abstract theology of his friends, Job inserts into his theological speech the reality of pain and suffering that hits the poor.

It is possible to say that the starting point of the friend's theology is distinct. They accept what the ancient had taught and, consequently, they cannot admit that God is unfair: "Does God pervert justice? Does the Almighty pervert what is right?" (8:3). This way, any contrary evidence simply needs to be apparent. Instead, Job, speaks from his own and the travelers' experience and understands it as a great injustice. If the traveler's testimony is reliable, the entire argumentation scheme proposed by his friends about the destiny of the wicked is completely false. God does not punish the wicked!

The friends' speeches go from Job's particular case to the general conditions of humanity and return. The official theology of reward governs their judgment about Job's case: he must be evil to fit in the scheme they have about things. The friends view Job's specific sufferings through the lens of their general theory of suffering. On the other hand, in Job's speech, the particular misfortune governs his vision of the general conditions; his unfair suffering opens his eyes for the patent injustice in the society in general.

Job condemns the theological speech of his friends till the end, by accusing them of giving him an empty and fake solace. The necessity to protect religion and the good image of God (15:4; 8:3; 4:17) converted them into betrayers of their friend. After refuting his friend's arguments, one by one, Job exclaims: "So how can you console me with your nonsense?" (21:34). The word *hebel*, used in this verse, means "waft," "emptiness." It is like the wind blowing, something as inconsistent as the morning fog dried out by the sun; or as some cloud carried through the air by the wind, or even as morning dew that evaporates at the first signs of heat. It is a word that marks the nature of the consolation and the theology offered by his friends. After listening to their speeches, Job is convinced that he is before the solid false appearance of a theology that uses all the benefit of tradition's weight but, when confronted by life experience, is reduced to waft, emptiness, and mistaken vanity. Can nonsensical words serve as solace?

It is worth transcribing Job 24:2–14 literally, for, according to Gutierrez, it represents a very detailed description that shows careful attention to the concrete situation of the poor.[8] In a text of clear prophetic inspiration, Job presents a list of facts that testify against justice and that God should either know or reject: theft of property, stealing cattle, attack on widows and orphans, and the hard description of the poor's conditions. This list of social oppressions is presented as a clear violation of the covenant with Israel, many times denounced by the prophets: The misery of the poor who do not have a place to be sheltered from the punishing weather; the oppressor who forces the poor to live without clothes and makes the hungry carry firewood; or rather, the worker in the fields who harvests the grain but has nothing to eat and yet the one who treads the winepress but cannot ease his thirst.

The destiny of the wicked (as described by the ancient wisdom tradition and that pleases the friends), does not fit in with Job's speech. His words insistently declare that the wicked oppressed the weak and God does absolutely nothing. After writing what happens in the fields, Job began to show that the situation is not better in the cities: "In the cities, the dying people groan" (Job 24:12). That is a particular and anguishing situation that gets worse because God does not hear their outcry. God remains deaf to the victims to whom Job shows solidarity. Before this scenario, Job concludes that God does not interfere in men's history, as he should do in order to reduce their crimes. It is also necessary to observe that the poverty described is not a result of destiny or inexplicable causes; those responsible for it are named without pity. Job 24:2–14 is describing a state of affairs caused by the wickedness of those who exploit and rob the poor.

> The wicked move boundary-marks away. They carry off flock and shepherd. They drive away the orphan's donkey. As security, they seize the widow's ox. The needy have to keep out of the way. Poor country people have to keep out of sight. Like wild desert donkeys, they go out to work. Searching from dawn for food. And in the evening for something on which to feed their children. They go harvesting in the field of some scoundrel. They go pilfering in

8. Ibid., 33.

the vineyards of the wicked. They go about naked, lacking clothes. And starving while they carry the sheaves. Two little walls, their shelter at high noon; Parched with thirst, they have to tread the winepress. They spend the night naked, lacking clothes. With no covering against the cold. Mountain rainstorms cut them through. Unsheltered, they hug the rocks. The orphan child is torn from the breast. The child of the poor is exacted as security. From the towns come the groans of the dying. And the gasp the wounded crying for help. Yet God remains deaf to prayer! In contrast, there are those who reject the light: Who know nothing of its ways and who do not frequent its path. When all is dark the murderer leaves his bed to kill the poor and needy. During the night the thief goes on the prowl, breaking into houses while the darkness lasts.

Job speaks on behalf of those who are the victims of society. The sufferers are not vagabonds or lazy people not wanting to work, as many people hastily think. Actually, they are poor even though they work and struggle to guarantee their subsistence. They work amid abundance, even though they suffer by having nothing to eat or to wear and no place to live. At the time that the Book of Job was written, poverty and misery were a result of a double tribute—internal (Judean) and external (Persian)—as we have already mentioned.

So, the victims of injustice are the orphans, the widows, the poor, and the hungry. In the Book of Job, as in the entire Old Testament, there is a social conscience that many modern readers do not have. God is the savior of the poor because the rich and powerful do not need salvation; they already own everything they want for living. John F. Alexander has observed that "the fatherless, widows, and foreigners each have about forty verses that command justice for them. God wants to make it very clear that, in a special sense, He is the protector of these weak ones."[9]

The difference between Job and the speech of his advisers is that they want and demand clarity and order from the Universe. They want to foresee what God will do, while Job wants to see God. They want to preserve a world of correct and coherent ideas and their theology. Job, however, wants to preserve his relationship with God. We see in Eliphaz's, Bildad's, Zophar's, and Eliuh's dialogues that they constantly and insistently talk *about* God. But the only one who talks *to* God is Job. Out of his intense pain and depression (he is on the edge of despair, if not actually in despair throughout the entire book) Job breaks through to address God.

9. Alexander, *Bible*, 57.

The great lesson from God's answer in Job's speech is that he asks justice to be understood not as a punishment to the wicked and a reward to the righteous, but as a communal search for a better life with plain freedom for everyone.

Yahweh was telling Job that this world is not the reign of perfect justice. There are proud and unfair people who succeed, just like Job denounced in his speech. But Yahweh also said that if Job could govern the world better, he pleasantly would offer Job such a task. On the highest level of irony, it is obvious that Job, as a mere human being, is not able to govern the world. On the second level of irony we observe the tragic fact that not even Yahweh is able to do it the way Job demanded; that is, with perfect justice. It seems that the Book of Job breaks any conception of harmony in creation. Creation is a conflicting and complex space and, because of that, it is not immune or exempt from adverse forces. Therefore, a fundamental question needs to be asked: Why can't we accept the fact that this life is imperfect? Saying that everything works well in this world created by God might be restorative for the casual viewer, but it represents a true insult for the one who is distressed and unhappy. Expressions such as "Don't be discouraged! Things happen to someone because they simply have to happen," certainly are not very encouraging messages to someone who is defeated and suffering.

I believe that Job has not realized the implications of Yahweh's historicity. A historical God in a historical world cannot avoid the necessity to opt between the real alternatives established by the present time and these alternatives not always include an option of perfect justice. Job realizes that in this historical world the alternatives are not always presented as "yes" or "no." So being a person means to accept historical conditions that sometimes seem unacceptable or, at least, accept them as starting points and struggle to make them better. The new thing about Job's apprenticeship can be described as follows: The expectation of complete justice in a world where not everything is justifiable is a real mistake. Therefore, it is this mistake that Job regretted.

Job's speeches vehemently condemn his friend's behavior and their theological speeches as well. Their answers are misplaced; they are theologically and sociologically dislodged for they try to force Job to renounce his own existence. As a matter of fact, the answers given by the theology of Job's friends are the usual answers the rich have given the poor and the healthy have given the sick. That is why Job sees no progress in their speeches. The official theology—represented by his friends—brings no new ideas. So Job questions the fundaments of that predominant theology. In doing so, however, Job never declares that God is unfair!

It is interesting to note that, since the beginning of the narrative, both the author of the text and God himself agree that Job is a God-fearing person (1:1 and 1:8). However, Job's personal problem is completely ignored. Nothing is said about guilt, nothing is said about innocence or about the meaning of suffering. God gives no answer, maybe because he represents Job's integrity. Maybe Job represents an image of true enlightenment: He does not possess God as a product or an attainment, but God possesses him.

When we recall what Job and his friends said about God, we can see that Yahweh's words to Eliphaz sound as a true confession of fault. After all, Job had said that God pursued him without reason or mercy. He had also declared that both the fortune of the righteous and the wicked was equal. His friends, however, defended the divine providence by assuring that the wicked who suffered deserved punishment from the Judge of the Universe. But this time Yahweh speaks to Eliphaz and sides with Job in the debate! The only thing that was left to Yahweh is doing justice to Job before his pious and false friends. He was not able to nullify the historical evil produced by his argument with Satan, but, at least, he was able to clarify the things between Job and his friends. God disqualifies his own defenders, while Job—the one who criticized the sapient and traditional order and anti-theology—is approved!

Yahweh does not give Job a strategy or a pattern, but simply a promise: "I am with you." God shows solidarity while the theology of Job's friends refrain any act of solidarity. A theology that refrains solidarity is like an anti-theology for it denies the very example of God. The Bible specifically commands believers to imitate God's special concern about the poor and oppressed. In the Old Testament, Yahweh frequently reminded the Israelites of their former oppression in Egypt when He commanded them to care for the poor: "God's unmerited concern about the Hebrew slaves in Egyptian bondage is the model to imitate"[10].

Job's book is a story without a conclusion. There is no rational solution for his suffering as well as for the suffering of millions of poor people. The only possible solution will happen in history with God and Job participating together to transform the world, so that such things don't happen again.

10. Sider, *Rich*, 57.

3

The Theology of Prosperity

Is a theology that establishes prosperity and victory as irrefutable signs of the presence of God in a society marked by poverty, suffering, and defeat relevant to the church?

One name for this theology of reward in the postmodern ecclesiastic environment is the "theology of prosperity." This theology declares that God's plan for the individual is to make him happy, blessed, healthy, and prosperous, or rather, a successful person. So where does the difficulty lie in this claim? The difficulty lies in the very fact that, for this theology to work, if someone is not financially successful, healthy, and happy it is only because this person lacks faith, does not follow what the Bible says about the God's promises, and is involved with Satan, or rather, is living in sin.

One proponent of this theology, Kenneth Hagin, claims that Jesus spoke to him through a revelation: "If anybody, anywhere, will take these four steps or put these four principles (Say it, Do it, Receive it and Tell it) into operation, they will always receive whatever they want from me or from God the Father."[1] The believer confronts God, diminishing his sovereignty, and in doing so, presents himself as the one who defines God's will and not the opposite! God is seen as a commodity and is sought according to the believer's necessity. It reminds me of Rees' interesting words.[2]

> I would like to buy $3 worth of God, please; not enough to explode my soul or disturb my sleep, but just enough to equal a cup of

---

1. Hagin, *Zoe*, 35–36.
2. Weaver, *Having*, 104.

warm milk or a snooze in the sunshine. I don't want enough of Him to make me love a black man or pick beets with a migrant. I want ecstasy, not transformation; I want the warmth on the womb, not a new birth. I want a pound of the Eternal in a paper sack. I would like to buy $3 worth of God, please.

Theological proposals like this one are what make this doctrine so attractive because, according to Proença,[3] it raises the believer to a dominant position in which God is obliged to concede him prosperity. No one can deny that it is a well-constructed argument. Let us consider Macedo's words about it:

> He [Jesus] broke all the barriers that were between you and God and now he says—"Come back home, to the Garden of Abundance for which you were created, and live the abundant life that God lovingly desires for you . . . God wants to be our partner . . . The basis of our society with God is the following: what belongs to us (our life, our strength, our money) starts to belong to Him and what is His (blessings, peace, happiness, joy and everything that is good) starts to belong to us.[4]

In this relationship of reciprocity, according to Magalhães and Souza,[5] God feels obliged to fulfill his biblical promises in the believer's life. God becomes prisoner and hostage of his own word. An excerpt from Moltmann, though lengthy, is essential here:

> What is called modern multi-faith and multi-cultural society is nothing other than the total market society. Religions and cultures are on display in this market in just the same way as political options, commodities, and services. Religions become the spiritual services on offer in the religious supermarket of the modern world. Individual religious liberty is certainly a powerful protection for every person's own human dignity, but because of the typical Western concept of the consumer's freedom to choose or dispose, that same freedom has turned religion into commodity, where the customer is allegedly always right. They are on offer optionally, without obligation, and with discount as "religion light," like the offers on the shelves for esoteric literature in the bookstore. Everything is possible; nothing is taken seriously.[6]

3. Proença, *Magia*, 37.
4. Macedo, *Vida*, 85–86.
5. Magalhães and Souza, *Os pentecostais*, 85.
6. Moltmann, *God for a Secular Society*, 250–51.

Possessions, purchasing power, health, and wealth are presented, without hesitation, as testimonies of spirituality and loyalty to God. Faith in God is valued as a means to obtain health, wealth, happiness, success, and earthly power. Experiencing evil, in this case, results from a lack of faith and the inability to confess it, or from disobedience to God. In these circumstances the believer is also vulnerable to Satan's cruelty. In Proença's words if, by divine right, the believer is assured of health, financial prosperity, and social status, those that, for any reason, do not enjoy such privileges "either do not understand well the biblical teaching, do not have enough faith, or still remain under the influence of Satan."[7] Indeed, the poor man must deal with the terrible anguish of failure or of Satan's theft of the grace that had been designated for him.

I once witnessed an episode that clearly illustrates this situation: It was a Thursday evening and, during the service, the pastor invited those who had any physical ailment to stand before the altar. Among them was a young woman. The pastor asked her two questions: What was her problem and was she was faithful to God. She answered, and he began to try to cast out her sickness (which was deafness in one ear). After several attempts with no result, his answer to her was: "While I was praying, the Holy Spirit told me that you cannot be healed unless you confess your hidden sins." That evening, I saw that young woman leave the altar with an extra burden on her painful life: the burden of a guilty conscience, thinking that God wanted to cure her but was unable to because of her sins.

In this theology, health, wealth, and success always represent God's will for the believers. Consequently, if the believer is poor or sick, it is because he is a sinner! This theology teaches that poverty is demonic and God, as a rich and loving Father, wants to see his children healthy, prosperous, and rich. For Macedo "whoever lives out[side] of this dimension is also out[side] of the divine plan and urgently needs to discover it."[8] This theological standpoint is easy and simple.

Accusing the victim is a way to assure oneself that the world is better than it seems to be and that no one suffers without good reason. It makes everyone feel better, except the victims, who suffer doubly with their social condition added to their original disgrace. One way to give sense to

---

7. Proença, *Magia*, 87.
8. Macedo, *Vida*, 56.

human suffering is to assume that we deserve what happens to us; that, in some way, disgrace is a punishment for our sins. Certainly this kind of theology, or rather anti-theology, solves the matters for Job's friends, but does not solve Job's problems or the problems of the millions of Jobs that continue to be born.

It is time for modern people who idealize and preach the "theology of prosperity" to stop speaking about social justice, human rights, and about the abomination of illegally accrued wealth. For the wealthy and high-powered souls of the modern world, any theology that denies the prosperity gospel is evil. After all, a theology that establishes material possessions as the result of one's spirituality pleases no one so much as those who possess much.

We must raise the alarm so that Christianity does not risk losing its sensitivity to the suffering of human beings. Any theology that does not start with the suffering of the innocent will remain the language of Job's friends—annoying advisors who prefer to justify God rather than to be touched by the pain of a suffering brother. Certainly it is not God they are defending, but themselves and their theology. A theology cannot lead us out of history. Instead, it needs to guide us into history, to a responsible role in its transformation.

The doctrine of the "theology of prosperity" denies divine solidarity. It is not altruistic, but selfish; it does not favor solidarity, but fosters contention; it does not make life a gift, but a possession. Such theology defends the idea that the true Christian is predestined to win, being more than a winner in all spheres of life. For this theology, suffering denies God's presence. Where is God when we look at an environment full of misery? We face a theology that seeks personal and corporate privileges, that is indifferent to injustice that is an everyday presence in a great part of the world.

For Campos, this theology is suited for people who feel insecure or excluded as it mobilizes them. They are disgusted with life and disillusioned, but still maintain vague hopes. For them, Campos considers this "theology of prosperity" "an accommodation of the Pentecostal message on a new Occidental social-economical stage that yields no longer an ethics of saving and investment—as Max Weber wrote—but an ethics of consumption."[9] Note the perception of eternity in this theology. The value

---

9. Campos, *Why Historic*, 122.

of this theology is in the possibility to access, in this lifetime, the rewards that once were deferred until life after death. In the Middle Ages, the church—through its theological practice—promised heaven as a post-death life, that is, "out of history"; the theology of prosperity promises access to heaven "in history," or in this life.

Such theology is committed to satisfying the wishes of a clientele and not to proclaiming doctrines or historic traditions. In fact, what matters are results. Now, the question is how to satisfy the immediate wishes of a clientele that is unconcerned with the distant future. From this point of view, one does not have to wait until death and eternal life to fulfill one's hope.

A return to biblical values is essential. After all, in the biblical texts we find more emphasis on humanity than on prosperity. A theology of prosperity, on the contrary, reduces everything to economic terms. In light of the misery, economic restructuring, and anomie in many poor countries, there is great potential for continued growth of the theology of prosperity. One can argue that this theology has responded to the psychosocial wishes of people excluded from modern capitalism. For these people, no other utopia guarantees them a little dignity and the chance to participate in the results of economic development. Many may have been convinced by the rhetoric of capitalist life, which promised to deliver prosperity, health, security, and full employment through consumerism, but ultimately failed.

In this theology, blessings like healing, for instance, were provided in the atonement. Key biblical passages are understood to show that the believer has been freed from physical sickness no less than he has been freed from condemnation for sins (Isa 53:4–5; Matt 8:16–17; 1 Pet 2:24). Hagin[10] writes:

> Through natural human truth a person realizes that he is sick, that he has pain or disease. But God's Word reveals that "He Himself took our infirmities, and bare our sicknesses" (Matt 8:17), and that by His stripes we are healed (1 Pet 2:24). Isn't God's Word just as true one time as it is another? Isn't it just as true when you have sickness and are suffering as when you are well? By believing what your physical senses tell you, you would say, "I don't have healing; I'm sick." But by believing the truth of God's Word you can say, "I am healed. By His stripes I have healing."

---

10. Hagin, *Real faith*, 20.

We must reject as unscriptural the teaching, either explicit or implied, that faith is in its essence a human quality or work that we perform to cause God to provide what we desire.

From this doctrine of healing provided in the atonement, prosperity theology infers that healing is already available to us, and that now it is *entirely up to us* whether we experience healing or not. Again, Hagin's words lay this out:

> Although healing is manifested in the physical, it is really a spiritual blessing, because it is spiritual healing. God is not going to heal your body. He is not going to do one thing about healing you. He's already done all He is ever going to do about healing you. He laid on Jesus your sickness and disease. He has already done something about it. Jesus has already borne them and by His stripes "ye were healed." Get your believing in line with what God's Word says. Quit hoping.[11]

We are God's children, and God has abundant life and the wealth of the universe at his disposal. Why, then, are we not healthy and rich? According to the theology of prosperity, our life of poverty, sickness, and failure is a result of Satan's dominion over us. When humankind fell into sin, Satan became the legal god of this world, giving him power over us. Thus, the elementary truth is that Jesus' redemption frees us from Satan's dominion and restores His rightful rule over us. As Hagin puts it:

> Jesus, however, came to redeem us from Satan's power and dominion over us . . . We are to reign as kings in life. That means that we have dominion over our lives. We are to dominate, not to be dominated. Circumstances are not to dominate you. Poverty is not to rule and reign over you. You are to rule and reign over poverty. Disease and sickness are not to rule and reign over you. You are to rule and reign over sickness. We are to reign as kings in life by Christ Jesus, in whom we have our redemption.[12]

In different religions, it is quite common to hear from various ministries utterances such as: "God doesn't want his children to drive old cars; he wants them to drive Mercedes. God wants only the best for his children." But when this same ministries are criticized for living in opulence—in an impoverished country—the lifestyle is defended as a "commandment

---

11. Ibid., 25.
12. Hagin, *I Believe*, 53–54.

from Christ." Alcorn also gives the example of a "man of God" that stands before his audiences and rebukes the "spirit of poverty,"[13] assuring them of material prosperity.

There is a famous phrase from the theology of prosperity—"live like a king's kid"—that is very popular in circles where health and wealth are abundant, but it reveals a great irony. The actual the "King's kid" was Jesus and he lived a life exactly the opposite of what is meant by the phrase today; a life *without* material abundance. Born in lowly Bethlehem, raised in corrupt and despised Nazareth, part of a pious but poor family that offered two doves because they could not afford a lamb (Luke 2:24), Christ wandered the countryside dependent on others to open their homes, for he had none of his own. So "living like a king's kid" seems an ironic slogan to employ. Whatever king's kid the prosperity proponents are speaking of, it obviously *isn't* Jesus.

The theology of prosperity views the ascended heavenly Lord as its model rather than the descended earthly servant. But Jesus warned his disciples not to follow a lordship model of power and authority, but to follow his own servant model: "Not so with you. Instead, whoever wants to become great among you must be your servant, and whoever wants to be first must be slave of all. For even the Son of Man did not come to be served, but to serve, and to give his life as a ransom for many" (Mark 10:43–45).

The basic problem with the theology of prosperity is that it is man-centered rather than God-centered. Alcorn says: "When approached from the prosperity posture, prayer degenerates into coercion, where we 'name it and claim it,' and keep on pulling his leash till God comes through."[14] This kind of persistence is not the kind Jesus encouraged, but an attempt to arm-twist the Almighty into increasing comforts and underwriting lifestyles about which we see no need to consult him about in the first place.

It can be said that "faith" becomes a crowbar to break down the door of God's reluctance, rather than a humble and subservient attempt to give thanks and to discern and lay hold of his will. Instead, we have predetermined that our will is God's. Consequently, we treat God as an object; a tool; a means to an end—the end we in our pseudo-sovereignty

---

13. Alcorn, *Money*, 102.
14. Ibid., 117.

have arbitrarily decreed to be best. Alcorn says that in the theology of prosperity God is seen as a great no-lose lottery in the sky, a cosmic slot machine into which you put a coin and pull the lever, then stick out your hat and catch the winnings while your "casino buddies" (in this case, fellow Christians) whoop and holler (or say "amen") and wait their turn in line.[15] They have forgotten that a crucial part of any faith is the investment of value in something durable rather than in the evanescent and endemically mortal individual life; in something lasting, resistant to the eroding of time, perhaps even immortal and eternal.

In this sort of theological system, the only reason for God's existence is to give us what we want. If we had no needs, God would probably just disappear. With this sort of twisted theology, prayer ceases to be sacred. Instead of a means to give him glory, prayer degenerates into an endless wish list to take before God.

I agree with Alcorn when he says that the theology of prosperity's view sees God as little more than a wish granter and, because of that, we cannot honestly call him "master" for we are the ones who are the masters. God becomes a genie but, instead of rubbing a lamp, we quote a verse or say "praise the Lord" three times and God will act out the script we have written for him.

From this standpoint, we cannot consider God's role in relation to us. A good theology must refuse a doctrine that instructs: "Put God to work for you and maximize your potential in our divinely ordered capitalist system."[16]

Our capitalist, pragmatic use of God demonstrates a clear lack of interest in God himself. After all, who cares what the genie is like? Genies serve one purpose—to grant our wishes and make us prosperous and happy. For many of us God is merely an object, instead of being the great subject of our faith. This attitude explains the glut of sermons, books, and articles written about us, and the dearth of those about God. God must be content and fulfilled to be at our service. Consequently, our genie is brought out and dismissed at our convenience. But as true Christians, is it even possible to say "You can go now, God. I'll call you back when I think of something else I want"?

---

15. Ibid., 117.
16. Ibid., 118.

In some ways, among some leaders' discourse, the theology of prosperity confirms a desire of accommodation with the Word: giving some believers the possibility of social status, and others the maintenance of the status they've attained, without the traditional "guilty conscience." Instead of hearing a message that says, "It is easier for a camel to go through the eye of a needle than for a rich man to enter the kingdom of God" (Matt 19:4), they can now enjoy possessions and wealth without constraints and with God's consent. So, for the fortunate, this theological approach brings relief; to the poor it promises the right, as God's children, to have or to get possessions—a first step toward granting the poor access to the consumer-driven society!

Believers of a theology that encourages consumerism find that the possession of personal wealth assures some certainties and exorcizes some fears. Maybe they are trying to find an escape from the agony called insecurity. If so, shopping becomes a daytime ritual to exorcize the gruesome apparitions of uncertainty and insecurity that haunt their nights. This represents a substantial change in the concept of spirituality: by buying products for what they represent—hopes and dreams, aspirations and pleasures—the buyer is searching for something beyond himself. This "reaching beyond himself" indicates a spiritual inclination in many of the everyday activities of shopping and in this way, buying becomes a spiritual experience. In fact, the shopping compulsion-turned-addiction is an uphill struggle against acute, nerve-wracking uncertainty and the persistent, stultifying feeling of insecurity. Bauman claims: "In consumer society, sharing in consumer dependency, in the universal dependency on shopping, is the *condition sine qua non* of all individual freedom; . . . above all, of the freedom to be different, to 'have an identity' . . . Identity—'unique' and 'individual'—can be carved only in the substance everyone buys and can get hold of only through shopping."[17]

This concept assumes that the one who does not buy is alienated, or rather, does not have an identity. His identity has been stolen and the only way to get it back is through consumption. In the religious language used by the theology of prosperity, Satan is among those who have caused this alienation and, consequently, poverty. In this sense, going shopping exorcises Satan and recovers one's stolen identity. Shopping turns us human and free. This association of illness, poverty, and failure with the

---

17. Bauman, *Liquid*, 84.

image of Satan allows the theology of prosperity to offer adherents an effective doctrine for times of suffering and uncertainty. Campos says: "the popular Brazilian image of Satan deems him the source of all the evil that attacks humans, animals or objects; hence, the importance given to exorcism, a way of blocking the forces that seek to prevent health, success and prosperity."[18]

In contrast to Job's experience—who after losing everything that he owned, fell to the ground and worshiped—disciples of the theology of prosperity conclude that when they lose their health and wealth they must have committed some unknown sin. But, if they can only find and confess it, they will regain their health and wealth.

Justified by isolated biblical passages, the theology of prosperity, as we see it today, is really a product of the capitalism and success-driven psychology that dominates industrialized nations, but also reaches poor ones. It is a product of our place and capitalistic time, and a reflection not of the Bible but of our own self-preoccupation.

I have given a lot of thought to the theology of prosperity, mainly when I have walked through the streets of Brazil's big cities, or when I have gone to churches and communities around our country and seen my brothers and sisters—believers in Christ—worshiping our Lord. I have pondered the theology of prosperity when I have sat with brothers and sisters that belong to or support popular causes like those dealing with homelessness, landlessness, abandoned children, etc.

The theology of prosperity does not begin with a wrong view of theology; it *ends* there. *It begins with a wrong view about God*, which produces a wrong view about humanity and a wrong view of worldly things.

This sort of theology will inevitably produce the kind of society increasingly evident in our days—a society of individualism, where people live parallel lives, never intersecting meaningfully with others. In this sort of society, independence is the only absolute, self-interest is the only creed, and convenience, expediency and profitability are the only values. In this sort of society people know the *price* of everything, but do not know the *value* of anything—people have a great deal to live on, but very little to live for. To counterbalance this exclusionary society promoted by individualism, a theology and a social practice that includes people is

---

18. Campos, *Why Historic*, 86.

necessary. In this sense, the Anglican Bishop Declaration[19] is important: "We believe that God created a good world for all persons. It is a world in which we are bound together in our common humanity, formed in God's image and in which each person has equal dignity and value. With immeasurable generosity, God has given bountiful resources for all to share. We are responsible to hold God's gift in trust for one another seeking the good for all."

While God created us to love and show solidarity to poor people and use things, this vision of individualism loves things and uses poor people. For example, the term "consumer" speaks not of a person, but of an economic unit. To a company, the consumer is only an object that can potentially contribute to its profit. However, mutuality and interdependence are a must if we are to live in a world where all people are respected and where the dignity and value of all God's creation are celebrated.

When God asked Cain where Abel was, Cain replied with another question, "Am I my brother's keeper"? Levinas's commentary on this passage is very relevant here. For this author, if we were in Cain's place, we should have said:

> Of course I am my brother's keeper; and I am and remain a moral person as long as I do not ask for a special reason to be one. Whether I admit it or not, I am my brother's keeper because my brother's well being depends on what I do or refrain from doing ... The moment I question that dependence, and demand as Cain did to be given reasons why I should care, I renounce my responsibility and I am no longer a moral self. My brother's dependence is what makes me an ethical being.[20]

The great burden of theology is to insist on *the moral priority of people* over institutions and their practices. It is people, not systems, who define the substance of justice and solidarity. This sense of justice and solidarity is essential for resisting the utter "commodification" of life. Consequently, any cultural force, social institution, or even theology that nullifies our sense of reality, justice, and solidarity is, practically speaking, atheistic and nihilistic. As appropriately claimed by Schweiker:

> The living God is never translatable into our system of signs, and morally speaking, this means that human worth, grounded in a

---

19. Stackhouse et al., *The Local*, 42.
20. Bauman, *The Individualized*, 72.

relation to God, cannot be commodified or measured within the discourse of any social sphere... Christian faith provides symbolic and conceptual means to think about the very presuppositions of economic justice in ways that can form human self-understanding around the integrity of life. It provides a bulwark against the tyranny of any social sphere and its practice—a wall rooted in the worth persons, consistent with a specific construal of the world.[21]

THE GENESIS OF THE THEOLOGY OF PROSPERITY

The terminology used to identify the theology of prosperity varies. Among its many names we stress: the Word-Faith Movement, the Health and Wealth Gospel, and Name It and Claim It. The beginnings of this movement can be traced to the writings of the radio preacher and Methodist minister William Essek Kenyon (1867–1948). He wrote approximately fifteen books in which he "stressed the power of words spoken in faith and the supremacy of a so-called revelation knowledge over knowledge obtained by the senses" (*Dictionary of Christianity in America*, 611). For him, the confession of positive faith brings God on the scene and compels God's action.

Kenyon's ideas directly influenced a number of preachers within the Pentecostal movement in the 1960s. The movement grew rapidly in the 1970s, in large part through the promotion of these preachers by the Trinity Broadcasting Network founded by Paul Crouch in 1973.

Kenneth Hagin has been among the best-known promoters of theology of prosperity teachings. His history, or how he found his theological "way," is at the very least curious: in the morning of August 8, 1934, Hagin was halfway through his sixteenth month as an invalid, confined to bed by an incurable heart deformity. Despite predictions that he could die any day, he had clung weakly to life. As he read the New Testament, his faith grew to the point where he believed God would raise him from his bed. But still nothing happened and he awoke each morning to another day of boredom and helplessness. But that morning would be different, as Hagin thought back to the verse that had sparked his faith: "What things so ever ye desire, when ye pray, believe that ye receive them, and ye shall have them" (Mark 11:24). "The having comes after the believing," he realized. "I've got to believe that my paralysis is gone while I'm still lying here flat

---

21. Stackhouse et al., *The Local*, 35.

on my back and helpless." So he did just that: instead of saying that he would be healed, he declared that he was healed."[22] An inner voice said to him: You believe that you are healed. If you are healed, then you should be up and out of that bed. Two days later he strode to the family breakfast table healed by this evidence of the power of faith in his own life.

In 1974 Kenneth Hagin founded the RHEMA Bible Training Center in Tulsa, Oklahoma, to offer training programs that included his teachings and practices. Hagin states that even though prosperity was a late addition to his doctrinal system, he did not learn it from any human teacher. But it did appear in Pentecostal evangelists whose prominence preceded Hagin's, most notably Oral Roberts. In 1955 Roberts published *God's Formula for Success and Prosperity*, his first book on this topic. In the 1960s Hagin embraced the prosperity message. Prosperity, especially financial prosperity, is also available to the believer who appropriates it by faith. Wealth, according to these preachers, was part of the blessing that Abraham received; while poverty was part of the curse that Christ canceled.

The following points are common to most theology of prosperity (Word-Faith) preachers:

1. Faith is a force, released by words, through which one can create reality. According to Copeland "The force of faith is released or activated by words. Faith-filled words put the law of the Spirit of life into operation."[23]

2. Speaking or positively confessing what one desires and requests from God activates the force of faith. Hagins says: "Your right confession will become a reality, and then you will get whatever you need from God."[24]

3. God wills every Christian to have financial prosperity. In fact, it is a right to be claimed by the Christian. In addition, poverty is not God's will for the Christian, but represents a Satan-defeated life.

4. God wills every Christian to have perfect health, and experience complete healing. God has obligated himself to heal every

---

22. Hagin, *I Believe*, 9–26.
23. Copeland, *The Force*, 18–19.
24. Hagin, *Right*, 30.

sickness of those who have faith. The promise of healing is part of Christ's atonement. Copeland claims, "God intends every believer to live completely free from sickness and disease."[25]

Indeed, the theology of prosperity is a systematization of the beliefs of the American middle class who faced the Great Depression in the 1930s. However, the theology of prosperity's roots are in the movements and therapeutic practices that emerged in the late twentieth century in the USA and Europe. Magalhães and Souza remind us that the theology of prosperity "can be considered a ramification of North American fundamentalism, which, after the crash of 1929, reoriented its ethics on behalf of a larger participation in public sphere."[26]

In Brazil, Proença places the advent of the theology of prosperity in the 1970s, a period when social conditions worsened in the country. The urbanization and modernization of the country; a mass rural exodus with its consequent poverty, violence, and existential and social instability and deep uncertainties were all elements innate to the period. Freston believes the Universal Church of the Kingdom of God was the principal port of entry to Brazil for a North American stream of Pentecostalism known as the "health and wealth gospel."[27] However, in Brazil, along with the Universal Church of the Kingdom of God, the theology of prosperity was also embraced by the following churches: Renascer em Cristo, Comunidade Evangélica Sara a Nossa Terra, Nova Vida, Bíblica da Paz, Cristo Salva, Cristo Vive, Verbo da Vida, Nacional do Senhor Jesus Cristo, Internacional da Graça de Deus e pelas organizações Adhonep e Missão Shekinah.

Would this expansion of the theology of prosperity mean the emergence of a new postmodern vision of Christianity? One could say that the theology of prosperity is the expression of a desire for power or simply a replica of European postmodern religiosity, which excludes and ignores the very core of theology: the protection and defense of human life. Doubtless, the theology of prosperity is a type of theology that best fits in a consumer-driven society.

Although the impoverished also live in an environment saturated by the fruits of modernity, they do not fully embrace the ideology of

25. Copeland, *Welcome*, 25.
26. Magalhães and Souza, *Os pentecostais*, 86.
27. Freston, "*Visão histórica*," 140.

human progress, because that progress has never quite reached them the same way it has the wealthy. Many poor are restless theologians seeking to discern who God is for themselves by knocking on both old and new doors until they find the theology—*kerygma*—that speaks to their situation with an outlook on reality that attests to "being" over "non-being." Concrete indicators of "being" are most notably items relating to health, family, work, and community.

Nevertheless, postmodern theology cannot ignore suffering, poverty, and inequality, which have never before been experienced as they are presently. It should propose models of church and Christian behavior that respond to the needs of the people, especially the needs of the victimized.

How we determine truth and falsehood and what we determine them to be relates directly to humanity's freedom for history and history's freedom for humanity. According to Alves, "If history becomes definitely closed to man, or man definitely closed to the future; if repression becomes the ultimate fact and domestication the ultimate determination of man's subjectivity, then we can say that the language of freedom no longer can be spoken."[28] In this, the poor become prisoners of a theological system, the keys for which have been thrown into the sea by the theologians themselves.

PENTECOSTALISM IN BRAZIL

When we talk about the theology of prosperity it is important to know how it emerged in Brazil. In order to do so, we must discuss the beginning of Pentecostalism in Brazil. And so, how did Pentecostalism start in Brazil?

Paul Freston describes the spread of Pentecostalism in Brazil as a series of waves.[29] *The first wave* occurred from 1910 to 1950, mainly among pioneer churches (Assembly of God and Christian Congregation of Brazil) and had as its framework the major internal migration of the period. For almost half a century these were the only forms of Pentecostalism known in Brazil, except for the Adventist Church of the Promise (1938), which fell outside the mold of historic Protestantism. The Pentecostalism of the first wave grew slowly in Brazil until the end of World War II. According to Campos, in the 1930s, Brazil had little industry and was

28. Alves, *Theology*, 168.
29. Campos, *Teatro*, 51.

a predominantly rural country.[30] Only 25 percent of its population lived in cities. This percentage grew to 36 percent in 1950, 68 percent in 1980 and 75 percent in 1990. Consequently, the internal migration gave a great push to the expansion of Pentecostalism.

The second wave was from 1950 to 1970. A defining factor of this wave was the fragmentation of Pentecostalism, especially within the city of São Paulo (Foursquare Gospel Church, Brazil for Christ Church, God is Love Church, Pentecostal Church, The House of Blessing, the Wesleyan Methodist Church, and many other smaller denominations). Pentecostalism in this period principally emphasized miracles, divine healing, and speaking in tongues. The unique background of the second wave shows us clearly that this new message was better suited to reach the lowest strata of urban society.

At the end of World War II, Brazil's political, economic, and cultural situation underwent profound changes: democracy took hold once again, industrialization was taken up anew, the steel industry grew quickly, and the European cultural influence gave way to a North American one. The nationalistic populism of President Getulio Vargas was replaced by the optimism of Juscelino Kubistchek, who opened the country to foreign industries. Despite the later political and economic problems—the military coup of 1964—the country continued growing: communication networks expanded and new roads in all regions of the country reduced distances. However, the gap between rich and poor increased when industry could not absorb all the labor generated by the intense rural exodus. It was a time of economic recession in all underdeveloped countries. In the cities, the crowds of poor people hoping for miracles were increasing, made up mostly of immigrants from the Northeast and from the interior of the South and Southeast.

The third wave, according to Campos, "coincided with an unprecedented economic crisis set off by the international petroleum crisis and was worsened by the inability of the Brazilian military dictatorship to resolve the basic problems of the poorest people."[31] *The third wave* began at the end of 1970s, strengthened through the 1980s, and was centered in the city of Rio de Janeiro (the Salon of Faith, Universal Kingdom Church, God's Grace International Church and other independent communities).

30. Ibid., 72.
31. Ibid., 71.

A defining characteristic of third-wave Pentecostalism was its skilled use of mass communication media. To Campos "it successfully penetrated the radio and television networks the military regime had set up to promote national security and to encourage the cultural unification of the country."[32] It is important to note that the third wave brought "the electronic church" to Brazil, a variety of Pentecostalism that has been successful in the U.S and Central America. The so-called third wave reflects the displacement of traditional culture and institutions by the arrival of the postmodern era. The emergence of these new churches was clearly a result of the globalization of both the country's and the world's economy and culture.

One man would influence all further pioneers of Brazilian Pentecostalism: the Baptist minister William H. Durham. He is said to have been baptized in the Holy Spirit on March 1907, during a visit to a mission on Azusa Street in Los Angeles, becoming from that moment on a devoted preacher of the Pentecostal message. His principal belief was of the sufficiency of Christ. For him, the experience of being baptized by the Holy Spirit should not be understood as a "second blessing" nor even as a sanctification. For him, Christ completed his work on the cross. Durham's influence on the first Pentecostal communities in Brazil is singular and, therefore, it is necessary to briefly describe some of these religious institutions:

The Christian Congregation of Brazil was the first Pentecostal denomination to arrive. Its founding leader was L. Francescon, an immigrant Italian whose work began at the Italian Presbyterian Church in the United States. However, seeing as he also spent some time at the Valdense Church, some authors disagree about his original religious beliefs. What is clear is that it was his Presbyterianism that instilled in him a belief in predestination. This belief was so intense that the church he founded does not evangelize. Instead, on days of baptism, it waits for the elect (the predestined) to come forward, and the person baptizing submerges those who do in the water without any inquiry into their faith. They believe that only the true elect would remain in faith. As a result, there is practically no place for a sophisticated message at the Christian Congregation of Brazil: the use of mass media, evangelistic campaigns, and literature to spread their message is banned.

---

32. Ibid., 72.

In addition to the Italian Presbyterian Church, L. Francescon also attended meetings led by C. F. Durham. In one of these meetings, Francescon received the gift of speaking in tongues and a revelation that he was to proclaim God's Word. So, he left the United States for Buenos Aires, Argentina, and Brazil. In Brazil he settled among other compatriot immigrants. Francescon's Christian Congregation in Brazil emerged in 1910 from a schism caused by one of his sermons during a service in a Presbyterian church. In its earliest stages, the Christian Congregation of Brazil was basically characterized as a church of immigrants for immigrants, becoming an ethnic church in the Pentecostal movement. During its first twenty years, the sermons at the Christian Congregation of Brazil were preached in Italian, and only after that, in Portuguese, the local language.

The Christian Congregation in Brazil developed mainly in the states of São Paulo and Paraná. Paulo D. Siepierski hypothesizes that the development of this church followed the commercial coffee route.[33] It is an accepted fact that at the turn of the twentieth century many immigrants were arriving in Brazil to replace the now abolished slave labor. Among them there were a great number of Italians who settled in the states of São Paulo and Paraná, where the soil was more suitable for agriculture, which led the Christian Congregation of Brazil to establish itself as a rural church, at least in the beginning.

Campos lists these influences that Francescon left on the Christian Congregation of Brazil:

a. Emphasis on illumination: seeking direct revelations from God;

b. Emphasis on speaking in tongues;

c. Rejection of bureaucracy and formal organization;

d. Distrust of theology and culture;

e. High value placed on purity of behavior;

f. Resistance to involvement with other denominations;

g. Strong apolitical views.

The Assembly of God, according to some authors, was founded by D. Berg and G. Vingren, two Swedish immigrant workers. Apparently they moved to the United States in the early twentieth century due to a crisis

---

33. Ibid., 79.

in their own country. Looking for a better quality of life, they settled in Chicago and eventually discovered meetings led by C. F. Durham. There, they received the baptism of the Holy Spirit as well as a revelation telling them to leave to "Pará," a state in Northern Brazil. Although many authors argue that D. Berg and G. Vingren went to Pará by chance, not for a specific missionary call, it is important to remember that, during that time, this state of Brazil was very popular abroad for its rubber latex production.

At the end of the 1910s, when these two missionaries arrived in Brazil, the country was at the peak of the "rubber cycle," a phenomenon that attracted thousands of people from other regions to the North of Brazil in a search for a "land without ailments." The North became the principal alternative for many Northeasterners who faced long periods of drought in their region, and as a result had been laid off by large landowners. Later, when the Asian market began to compete with Brazilian rubber latex, the frustrated adventurers instigated a backwards-migratory flow. Following this flow, the Assembly of God established churches in Brazil in the opposite direction of the Christian Congregation. Initially, while the latter occupied the South and Southeast; the former occupied the North and Northeast regions. Both ended up occupying other regions of the country. The establishment of the Christian Congregation followed the coffee route; while the Assembly of God followed the rubber latex route and its reverse population flow.

The Assembly of God also emerged from a schism inside a traditional Protestant church, the Baptist Church of Belém (the capital of Pará). D. Berg and G. Vingren settled at the Baptist church and were given many opportunities to preach. During a prayer meeting led by one of them, a woman received the gift of speaking in tongues and became the first believer in that church with this gift. This provoked an uproar in the church and began an increasing exclusion of those who insisted on using this gift. The Swedish missionaries' interpretation of the Bible caused a polemic among the Baptists. The doctrine of the Holy Spirit—speaking in tongues as an evidence of the baptism of Holy Spirit—was the central dispute between them and the local leaders of the Baptist church. As a result, nineteen people left to form the Assembly of God.

The Foursquare Gospel Church was founded by Amy Semple McPherson. It is said that she experienced a divine healing during one of W. H. Durham's meetings and began spreading the word about her experience. Although she was a contemporary of other Brazilian Pentecostalism pioneers, her church didn't arrive in Brazil until the middle of the twentieth century. Unfortunately, by that time she had already passed away.

It is possible that this church came to Brazil from the United States as result of the "National Evangelization Crusade" promoted by H. William and R. Bootright, preachers of divine healing. Some traditional Protestant churches, among them an Independent Presbyterian Church in São Paulo, opened their doors to this National Crusade. Its doctrine not only created problems and discord in the church, it led to the emergence of the Foursquare Gospel Church. William was supported by twenty pastors, most of them from other denominations, mainly the Methodist and Assembly of God. Initially, they gathered in large tents—which would become the evangelistic and missionary model adopted by the Foursquare Gospel Church—and explored salvation, supernatural experiences such as the baptism of the Holy Spirit and divine healing, and reaffirmed the return of Christ. Often, these pastors left their denominations, taking congregants with them to join this new ministry that was attracting so much attention. The Foursquare Gospel Church played a fundamental role in the emergence of national Pentecostal churches such as Brazil for Christ, God is Love. Its influence even reached the Universal Church of the Kingdom God. In Freston's evaluation: "In the beginning . . . the importance of Foursquare Gospel Church was restricted to the role it played during the 50s, that was, to import more suitable religious techniques for a new mass society. Later, in a parallel process of replacing import, just like the country was living, these techniques were learned and adapted by natives . . . divine healing itself was no longer a novelty, but its extensive use and practice in public places was."[34]

Ricardo Mariano proposes the following classifications for Pentecostalism, based on the theory of three waves: Classic Pentecostalism, Deutero-Pentecostalism, and Neo-Pentecostalism.[35] Three prospects characterized the new Pentecostal churches (Neo-Pentecostal): the "war against the Devil," the "theology of prosperity," and the "liberation of the traditional practices and customs of Pentecostal sanctity."

34. Campos, *Why Historic*, 29.
35. Freston, "*Visão histórica*," 113.

Neo-Pentecostalism is specifically characterized by the adoption of a relationship between the believer and God in which the former has the right to enjoy the best things this world can offer. Through this, its doctrine encourages believers to enjoy new technologies, accumulate more and more wealth, live better, own the best car, consume more and, above all, set aside feeling guilty for enjoying the world instead of denying it. It is noteworthy that ascetic behavior has been decreasing among Neo-Pentecostal groups.

Monteiro observed that old religious systems were disintegrating and "almost entrepreneurial models of conduct, differentiated more by labels and packaging than by the products they offer,"[36] were emerging. Alves argues that an entrepreneurial mentality and capitalist logic can best explain the success of these enterprises, which specialize in the transaction of spiritual goods and fall within a philosophy of the exchange of values.[37]

THE MCDONALDIZATION OF THEOLOGY

Based on the above discussions, we should ask: doesn't the theology of prosperity lead us to the McDonaldization of theology? Isn't it this discourse about God that leads to a consumerist theology? A "theology to go"? Spiritual consumers are free to shop around in their search to improve upon or supplement what they already have. With a mobile theology, one searches unceasingly for new and innovative spiritual experiences.

However, it is necessary to explain the concept of McDonaldization as well as its influence on theology. George Ritzer developed the McDonaldization concept in his book *The McDonaldization of Society*. For him McDonald's is the major example—the paradigm—of a wide-ranging process called McDonaldization, which is: "the process by which the principles of the fast-food restaurant are coming to dominate more and more sectors of American society as well as of the rest of the world."[38] The importance of this McDonaldization process can be seen in many instances. I mention only one as an example: the annual "Big Mac Index" published by the prestigious magazine, *The Economist*. It indicates the purchasing power of various currencies around the world based on the

---

36. Mariano, *Neopentecostais*, 23–49.
37. Monteiro, "*Igrejas, seitas*," 52.
38. Alves, "*A empresa de cura*," 61.

local price (in dollars) of the Big Mac Sandwich. The Big Mac is used because it is a uniform commodity sold in many (115) different nations.

We must look at the effects of McDonaldization not only in the restaurant business but also in every other aspect of society. Ritzer writes: "The McDonaldization thesis involves far more than restaurants; universities, churches, and museums, among many other settings, can be seen as becoming McDonaldized. Almost no sector of society is immune from McDonaldization, and this means that innumerable aspects of people's everyday lives are transformed by it."[39]

Even more, McDonaldization has shown every sign of being an inexorable process, sweeping through seemingly impervious institutions and regions of the world.

Ritzer presents four areas on which he bases the success of this model. The four areas offered to consumers, workers, and administrators are: efficiency, calculability, predictability, and control. Drane points out that it is not difficult to see these marks in the church environment and consequently in their influence on theology. After all, he says, "we love rationalized systems and try to apply them to everything from our theology to the way we welcome visitors to our Sunday services."[40] Let us examine these areas more closely:

Efficiency

This critical element of McDonald's success is discovering the optimum method for getting from one point to another. For consumers, McDonald's offers the best available way to get from being hungry to being full. Their efficiency fills many other needs as well. Organizational rules and regulations help ensure highly efficient work. In a society that venerates a McDonaldized lifestyle, a prepackaged theology can be an attractive option. It is the spiritual equivalent of fast food, and unlike the home-prepared meal, it requires no preparation, no cleaning up afterwards, and no involvement in cooking it. The key to efficiency in the theology of prosperity is being able to process as many people as easily as possible. But true theology is not about processing people as though they are peas in a pod.

---

39. Ritzer, *McDonaldization*, 201.
40. Ibid., 202.

McDonaldized theology transforms God into the ultimate mall—an extremely effective selling machine. If consumer spending clearly becomes far more efficient for the consumer by placing virtually all shops in one location—the mall—there is nothing better than placing in God the answers for all the problems related to consumerism. Efficiency is clearly advantageous to consumers (believers), who can obtain what they need more quickly with less effort. In a McDonaldized society, people rarely search on their own for the best means to an end. Rather, they rely on previously discovered and institutionalized means. A good illustration was the Vatican's announcement on radio and TV in 1985, saying that Catholics could receive indulgences (a release from certain forms of punishment resulting from sin by way of devotional practices) through the Pope's annual Christmas benediction.[41]

One can see that efficiency accordingly leads to a simplification of the final product. According to Ritzer, for fast-food restaurants, complex foods based on sophisticated recipes are not the norm.[42] The staples of the industry are foods that require relatively few ingredients and are simple to prepare, serve, and eat. As for theological discourse, it is simpler to determine what we desire from God's hands by using previously memorized expressions: Say it, Do it, Receive it, and Tell it. Or we could compare this situation to many businesses these days, where, instead of dealing with a human operator, people must push a bewildering sequence of numbers and codes before getting to the extension they want.

Another mechanism for increased efficiency in a McDonaldized world is putting customers to work. In the theology of prosperity version, God is placed at our service. There's nothing more efficient than the Almighty acting according to our desires.

Calculability

This is emphasizing the quantitative aspects of products sold and services offered. In McDonaldized systems, quantity has become equivalent to quality. A lot of something means it must be good. The most important result of calculability is the ability to produce and obtain larger amounts of things very rapidly.

---

41. Drane, *The McDonaldization*, 151.
42. Ritzer, *McDonaldization*, 133.

Theology is not immune to this obsession with numbers and quantity. However, we need to be aware of the limitations of numbers, because while they are the easiest way to measure, they are a blunt instrument and often have little to do with what is really happening. We live in a dangerous kingdom of calculating, counting, and quantifying. Inside this kingdom we are what we possess; the more the better.

Theological calculability is a particularly irrelevant and unproductive way to stifle the human life and values needed to construct a healthy society. Its result is the creation of dehumanizing structures. People's success is defined by the quantity and value of the objects they possess and can afford to buy. Therefore it becomes necessary to multiply the number of books that try to teach the believer how to find the fastest and easiest way to success. Reducing human beings to mere objects compromises life and sets up death as a daily referential. Erich Fromm authoritatively spells out this scenario:

> While life is characterized by growing in a structural and functional way, the necrophile individual loves everything that does not grow; everything that is mechanic. The necrophiliac is moved by a desire for converting what is organic into inorganic, for looking at life mechanically as if other people were things. All the processes, feelings, and thoughts of life become things. Memory not experience; possessing not being is what matters. The necrophile individual can feel fulfilled with an object—a flower or a person— only by possessing it. As a result, a threat to this possession is a threat to himself. If he loses possession he loses the contact with the world.[43]

The emphasis put on quantification creates the illusion of quality. According to Ritzer, in "a society that emphasizes quantity, goods and services tends to be increasingly mediocre."[44] It is an illusion equivalent to McDonalds' illusion, where it is possible to get more food while paying less. Immersed in this illusion, we emphasize quantity. Without a doubt, it encourages us to avoid the reality that surrounds us and in exchange offers us another supposed reality, a delusion disguised as reality.

Calculability generates a theological doctrine without depth simply because it produces in the poor believer the delusion that he can consume more in a society in which he is confined to the periphery.

43. Ibid., 137.
44. Fromm, *El corazón*, 28–29.

Predictability

This is the assurance that products and services will be the same in all places at any time. The workers in McDonaldized systems also behave in predictable ways. They follow corporate rules as well as the dictates of their managers. In many cases, what they do, and even what they say, is highly predictable. It is like a script they have to follow. It is enough to memorize and follow the rules no matter the situation. To achieve predictability, Ritzer says, "A rationalized society emphasizes discipline, order, systematization, formalization, routine, consistency, and methodical operation."[45]

In this sense, from the believer's point of view, predictability makes for peace of mind in day-to-day dealings. However, predictability establishes a barrier to creativity and innovation. Theologically speaking, the moment repetition becomes a behavioral tendency, it is no longer necessary to create anything. The human being stops taking part in his own existence; he stops creating and recreating and deciding about his own future. Consequently, eternal repetition is presented as the very substrate of theology and, by fixing in theology its roots, reduces it into empty speech.

Every theology has the tendency to transform itself into a system of power and repression against all kinds of creativity and criticism. But it is necessary to resist this repression. Theology is by necessity based on creativity and stimulates real actions and reflections on reality. In doing this, theology responds to human beings, calling to them when they are not authentic or committed to using their creativity to transform their own reality.

Fast-food restaurants tell and train employees what to say and do in various circumstances. This, in turn, makes customers' replies more predictable. Similarly, when theological discourse comes in a ready package, it is no longer necessary to think; you merely have to open the package and regurgitate its content. In this sense, theological discourse has the tendency to become petrified, lifeless. In fact, a constant concern with shaping and packing can actually become a strategy to ensure that nothing fundamental is going to change. We face an excellent strategy to maintain the *status quo*.

The theology of prosperity and its consequent system of accumulation—used as an instrument of immobilization—does not recognize

---

45. Ritzer, *McDonaldization*, 82.

humans as historical beings. As a result, as Schipani points out, "the prophetic function of the church is suppressed and its testimony, then, means fear of change and of radical transformation within an unjust world."[46] In this way, the theology of prosperity ends up being prescriptive; that is, it takes stories about success and how to achieve it, and puts them into a package to be sold to people as though God acted that way. It means people only need to follow precisely what this theology prescribes in order to achieve their objectives. Such theology speaks about reality as if it were static, divided into compartments, and predictable.

In Ritzer's words, "McDonald's pioneered the routinization of interactive service work and remains an exemplar of extreme standardization. Innovation is not discouraged . . . at least among managers and franchisees. Ironically, though, the object is to look for new, innovative ways to create an experience that is exactly the same no matter what McDonald's you walk into, no matter where it is in the world."[47] In the theological field, the believer simply knows that he will encounter a safe place, health, success, etc. He simply knows what he is going to get before he prays. The theological emphasis on predictability creates a constant pressure to homogenize our understanding of spirituality and human values; to homogenize not only products but people. So, according to Drane there is inevitably a temptation to process people so that they all turn out like clones of one another.[48] We can say that the goal of this kind of McTheology is, in many ways, to try to make believers look, act, and think more predictably. The concern, then, is this: inauthenticity is dangerous and denies a human the possibility of being more in a society that reduces him to less.

Faith becomes predictable, and even personal experiences are forced into a mold, so that in any given context one person's faith journey sounds much the same as another. This occurs when theology becomes made-to-order; when individuals hear of other people's experience and try to get the same for themselves.

Theology, however, cannot become predictable because, it, by its very nature, is a discussion of the *other* (God) and the defense of the *other*'s life (the human being). This kind of predictability sought by the churches—and their corresponding theology—denies and contradicts

---

46. Ibid., 83.
47. Schipani, *Conscientizacion*, 58.
48. Ritzer, *McDonaldization*, 18.

the unpredictability associated with God. It gives rise to the repression of alternative religions that are more mystical and unpredictable. After all, theology speaks about a God who is Spirit, and therefore, fluid.

Control

According to Drane, control is exerted over the people who enter the world of McDonald's. Lines, limited menus, few options, and uncomfortable seats all lead diners to do what management wishes them to do—eat quickly and leave.[49] Control is used to reduce variability. The more control that is imposed on human beings with their resulting passivity, the more they naively tend to adapt themselves to the world and the partial reality they are offered. So they accommodate themselves instead of trying to transform their reality as well as transform themselves. The result is truly dangerous: domestication and passivity not only take hold of the subject, but also the reality in which the subject lives. One might say that it is control that guarantees efficiency, calculability, and predictability: programming ourselves to accept specific results, and thereby not allowing room for something extraordinary, can easily become a subtle form of control.

Replacing humans with non-human technology further increases this control. Ritzer stresses: "technology includes not only machines and tools but also materials, skills, knowledge, rules, regulations, procedures, and techniques."[50]

From a theological perspective, control is exerted with the same objective: to create a theology for which thinking and decision-making are hardly ever necessary. A subject is better controlled and manipulated if he is not encouraged to reflect and be autonomous. Using Paulo Freire's terminology, this action can be called "banking education,"[51] which has as its goal a human being's domestication, not his freedom. This kind of education converts the human being into a passive subject and diminishes his human status. A human is transformed into a thing. He becomes merely an object, a repository. Consequently, his empty conscience is filled by worldly things, pre-digested by those in power, the residues of which control his conscience. Effectively, more and more people lose the opportunity, and perhaps the ability, to think for themselves.

49. Drane, *The McDonaldization*, 155.
50. Ibid., 18.
51. Ritzer, *McDonaldization*, 104.

We must not misunderstand: power and theology are closer than we might imagine as the latter can also be a type of control. According to Foucault, power cannot be owned as an object or a property that you may or may not possess.[52] There are not two sides: those who have power and those who are deprived of it. Strictly speaking, power does not exist; but only *acts* of power. Which is to say that power is something to be held, to be wielded, to be used. It is not an object but a connection.

For social scientists it is necessary to work with people's reflectibility because those who act are the ones who construct social reality for the rest. They do this by means of language actions, since all social actions are built from language actions. Júlia Miranda points out: "Although not every social reality is a speech, this view calls attention to quotidian speech (everyday speech) while analyzing the construction of collective subjects. In this sense, it is possible to follow the construction of the senses people from a certain group or class give to their reality, which contributes to identify the group itself and its objectives."[53]

Foucault's words speak for themselves:

> Power produces; it produces what is real; produces domains over objects and rituals of truth. Power has a productive efficiency, it is positive. And that is the very aspect that explains the fact that power has the human being as its target; not to torture and mutilate it, but to improve and tame it. What basically interests power is not to banish men from social life, by impeding them to exercise their activities, but to manage men's life, control them in their actions so that it is possible and viable to use them to their utmost, by taking advantage of their potentialities and by using a gradual and continuous improvement system of their capabilities. Such objective is at the same time economical and political: to increase the effect of their work, that is, turning men into a workforce by giving them economical utility; to reduce their capacity to rebel, fight, and protest against power orders; that is, turning men politically docile. To sum up: to increase the economical utility and reduce what is inconvenient and dangerous; to increase the economical force and reduce the political force.[54]

Many times our understanding of power compels us to see it as an object. This perception, however, makes power an obsession and creates

52. Freire, *La educación*, 20–21.
53. Foucault, *Microfísica*, 37.
54. Miranda, *Carisma*, 38.

a tyrannical view of power. Therefore, it is necessary to see power from where it originates, by looking at it as though it is a process, not an unchanging entity.

If this is correct then we can declare that power is not a thing but a connection; a connection between people who coexist in the same society; where all social relationships are relationships of power. And, here, power becomes a mutual influence. Primarily, power is at the foundation of society; it lies at the base of every social and human relationship.

I believe Foucault's question also applies perfectly to theology: What kind of power is this, with its ability to generate words of truth with such powerful effects in a society like ours? For Foucault, in the society we live:

> Multiple relations of power pass across, characterize, and constitute the social body; they cannot be dissociated, set off or function without production, accumulation, circulation, and functioning of a real discourse. There is no exercise of power without a certain economics of the discourses of truth, which works in this power, from it and through it. We are submitted by power to produce truth and we can only wield power by producing truth.[55]

After all, we are judged, condemned, classified, forced to work, destined to live or die a certain way, as a result of true or supposedly true dictates from the ones who are in control.

Foucault warns us not to see power as a solid and homogenous phenomenon, as if it were "a domination of an individual over others, a group over others, a class over others," and he adds we should:

> Keep in mind that power—except if we consider it from very high or very far—is not something to be shared with the ones who hold it, or keep it exclusively; or with those who do not hold it and are submitted to it. Power, I think, should be analyzed as something that circulates, or rather, as something that only works in a chain system. It will never be found here or there; it will never be in some people's hands; it will never be possessed as wealth or estate. Power works. It is exercised in a network and in such a network, not only the individuals circulate but they are also in a position to be submitted to this power and also to wield it. They will never be the inert or permissive targets of power; they are always its

---

55. Foucault, *Microfísica*, 35.

intermediaries. In other words, power passes by individuals, it does not apply on them.[56]

Using the same view as Foucault (when he declares that the bourgeoisie does not have an interest in the insane, but in the power exercised over them; or that the bourgeoisie does not have an interest in children's sexuality, but in the system of power that controls children's sexuality), we could also declare that certain kinds of theologies do not have an interest in believers but in the system of power that circulates among believers and controls them.

Individuals that are perceptive and aware are impractical subjects for theological control. Passive individuals are at the mercy of another's decision-making. For Freire "as banking education nullifies the learners' power or minimizes it, by stimulating their naivety not their criticism, it satisfies the oppressor's interests: for them, the world denudation of transformation is not fundamental."[57]

We know that the increasing individualism of people in modern society contributes to this new enslavement and consequently better control over them. "Divide and rule" was a proven Roman method of domination. And as Moltmann shows:

> If we want to rule over other people, we must separate them from each other as far as possible, isolate them, drive them apart, and individualize them. When in this division we arrive at the final and indivisible entity, that is the subjugated person per se. The modern individual is therefore the end product of the divide-and-rule method. What we have are individuals in an atomized world.[58]

As a result, the modern human being has become the target of division and a controllable subject for the powerful; he has developed an individualistic and materialist character, unaware of the reality that surrounds him. When the theology of prosperity encourages the believer to consume, it reinforces these characteristics in him instead of transforming him into a more conscientious and communal person. As a result, socially harmonious practices are replaced by individual well-being.

Therefore, conscientious individuals are dangerous to the "order" of a pre-established ideology, even a theological one. In this sense, the more

56. Foucault, *Em defesa*, 29.
57. Ibid., 43.
58. Freire, *Pedagogia*, 60.

one is aware, the easier he reveals his own reality and, consequently, the more he uncovers the essence of what he wants to know. Freire declares that "awareness cannot exist outside praxis . . . it is a historical commitment. It is also a historical conscience. It is a critical insertion in history and implies human beings to assume their role as subjects who make and remake the world."[59] So, it becomes apparent that any theological expounding that proposes a domestication of humanity is, in fact, proposing a dehumanizing action. Consequently, it stops being theology simply because it denies the life it was supposed to defend.

Perhaps the main task of the church and theology in a global future is educational. The church needs a theology that aims to develop the awareness and the critical attitude of believers, so that, as human beings, they will be able to choose and decide, instead of being submissive. They will be able to be reflexive, instead of tamed; active and not passive as the theology of prosperity too often encourages them to be. Churches and their theologies must be witnesses to the kingdom of God through teaching, learning, and living out justice.

One can compare the doctrine of the theology of prosperity to a panopticon. A panopticon is a circular prison with level upon level of cells facing in toward the center of the circle. From a single point inside this prison, guards can observe every moment of the prisoners and check to see if they follow the prescribed routine. The theology of prosperity itself ends up being simply "a deposit." The theologian makes the deposit and the believer is the bank. And, instead of proclaiming life, this theologian makes announcements that believers passively receive, learning and repeating them night and day. In this accumulative view of theology, all those who leave or break this routine are seen as violators of the preestablished order, one with a routine that must be rigorously followed. These theologians infer that following their prescribed steps eliminates most of the uncertainties of life.

It is critical to break away from a theology that fosters intimate relations with power. This model that Hobbes describes, for example, is certainly ill-fitting: "I signalize, at first, as a general tendency of all men a perpetual and restless desire for power and more power, which ceases only with death. And its cause is not that one not always expects a more intense pleasure . . . but the fact that power cannot be taken for granted

---

59. Moltmann, *God for a Secular Society*, 156.

without getting even more power."⁶⁰ So, it is not the power itself that is insane, but the human beings—the powerful—who are dominated by a compulsion, by an immoderate desire—the *libido dominandi*—who have an insane aggression—and in the end are divided and injured.

To escape from the submission and control of religious doctrine it is important to stress that the teaching-learning theological process assumes two viewpoints. The *society of knowledge and the construction of knowledge*. Through these, we come to understand that in many ways polysemy has been traded for monosemy. Orlandi stresses that "the meaning (meanings) of a speech escapes (escape) from the exclusive dominion of the speaker. So, we could say that every speech, per definition, is polysemic, and the authoritarian speech tends to stanch polysemy."⁶¹ As a power, monosemic theological doctrine fears any change that might threaten that power. And power never abdicates itself.

When theology frees the human being, it begins to see him as one who reflects on his own situation. The more he reflects on his reality, the more his conscience becomes committed to, and ready to intervene in, his reality in order to transform it.

---

60. Freire, *Conscientización*, 30.
61. Hobbes, *Coleção Os Pensadores*, 59.

4

Building Solidarity on the Road of Defeat

HUMAN BEINGS DO NOT LIVE BY VICTORY ALONE

THE THEOLOGICAL DOCTRINE THAT establishes the realm of victory and, consequently, the realm of prosperity as fundamentally divine, is not a new concept in history. The identification of victory, truth, and justice with those who dominate can be found, for example, in Flavius Josephus when he narrates General Agrippa's pronouncement to the Jews, attempting to dissuade them from starting a war against the Roman Empire: "If everyone who lives below the sky fears and honors the Roman's weapons, how do you want to start a war against them? . . . So, who will you take as partners for this war? . . . As there is not another help except God's and the Romans have Him too, because without His particular help, it would be impossible for such great empire to remain and be preserved."[1]

We are used to thinking from the viewpoint of the winners and victory. Such logic dictates that all who die early due to poverty or from an easily curable illness were predestined to fail. They are victims because they are defeated. They are defeated because the God of victory is not on their side.

By this logic, among the crowd of the defeated, God is with the victor. This seems to be the hermeneutical key used by Franz Hinkelammert when, analyzing the premiere of Handel's *Messiah* in London, he

---

1. Josefo, *La guerra*, 258–60.

associated it with the British troops marching to conquer India. The Messiah would be walking at a great pace to dominate the pagan forces in India. However, as Hinkelammert himself appropriately concludes: "Jesus was also in India but he was not beside that Messiah."[2] It is no surprise that since Constantine, this doctrine of the kingdom of God has been linked to the Christian Empire.

I think theology needs to be unshackled from "triumphalist," Western Christian history and to be opened again to the biblical accounts concerning the suffering of God's people. Moltmann stresses this idea saying: "the victors of history are untouched, apathetic, because they are almighty. They have no feeling for the sufferings of their victims because they are incapable of feeling guilt. Like their God, they are omnipotent and impassible."[3]

In this victorious vision, God himself is represented from the angle of those who wield social and economic power. From this fundamental reading, all other views are seen as inopportune and heretical. Through such a representation, God is seen as the representative of wealthy, domineering, victorious, and healthy people. Thus, both heaven and earth are controlled by the wealthy and powerful. Their gates are guarded and entrance is forbidden to ordinary people. The victim loses his rights in heaven as well as on earth. The loss of his earthly rights is nothing less than the very reflection of his heavenly reality. In this sense, God is no longer with the poor and the excluded, but against them!

Such a viewpoint forgets Bonhoeffer's words when he claimed that the Bible "directs [man] to the powerless and suffering God. [He] is weak and powerless in the world, and that is exactly the way, the only way, in which He can be with us and help us."[4] It is worth recalling Bonhoeffer's remarkable words from his personal experience in 1944 in a Gestapo cell when he discovered that "only the suffering God can help."[5]

Therefore, God is to be found not among the powerful but among those who are subjugated, who suffer, who are not given a future. However, we need to categorically make clear that he doesn't suffer because of masochistic tendencies, as there is no glory in suffering. On the contrary, God

---

2. Hinkelammert, *Sacrificios*, 39.
3. Moltmann, *God for a Secular Society*, 182.
4. Bonhoeffer, *Letters*, 219–20.
5. Ibid., 361.

suffers because he participates in the pain of those who are oppressed and hopeless.

We may be living in a time of theological accommodation; not only as a church accommodating the society that creates it, but also with a theology that alienates, instead of questioning that society. We are concerned with wealth, health, stability, famous brands, cars, and shopping. Because of that there is little social concern. However, in a world marked by violent acts on all levels—violence against people, against nature, and against the future of life—it's important to remember Moltmann's words: "Love for life and reverence for life must be newly awakened, so that they may confront the growing cynicism that is widespread in the countries . . . The protection of the life of the weak, the protection of the life of our fellow creatures, and the protection of the future of the life we share: these things must be reinforced, in order to counter the brutal structures of death."[6]

In the community of Jesus' disciples, theological doctrine was presented as an instrument that created communities, not by excluding the weak, but empowering them. Therefore, their experience is the very reverse of this perverse logic that provoked, in the historical scenario of human society, the birth of progress and poverty as twin brothers.

Jesus' outcry on the cross—"My God, my God, why have you forsaken me?" (Matt 27:46)—represents and reflects the outcry that all victims from this system have in their throats. One might even say it represents an extension of Job's outcry. Jesus' despair on the cross is the clearest expression of the despair felt by the poor, weak, and defeated. They identify themselves with such an outcry: "The cross is not the completion or justification of suffering, or the announcement of the final triumph of the ambiguities in history."[7] Jesus' life and suffering tell us that God is not separated from the trials of humanity. God is not aloof. He is not a mere spectator but is participating with us in our history. God is not merely tolerating or healing human suffering. God does not act in a vacuum.

The gospel is the announcement of the historical reality of the ongoing politics of God, which is expressed not as a philosophical or mystical experience, but rather, as a power that invades history. The New Testament communities confessed Jesus as a "servant" (John 13). So, the language of theology remains derived from history and committed to history. Alves

---

6. Moltmann, *God for a Secular Society*, 69.
7. Alves, *Theology*, 120.

says that Jesus must be understood as the power and as the standard of God's historical politics of human liberation.[8] Therefore, when we speak about Jesus, we are speaking about history, about the ongoing politics of grace throughout history and consequently about the triumph of human beings throughout history. Surely, we are not talking about the reduction of human beings to an economic value.

Through the Incarnation, we begin to perceive what God's identification with the weak, poor, and sick really means: "Though he was rich yet for your sake he became poor" (2 Cor 8:9). What a statement! God did not become flesh as a wealthy aristocrat—the very synonym of success. Sider characterizes this relation between success and defeat as follows: "God might have entered history as a powerful Roman emperor living in luxurious power at the center of the greatest empire of the time. Or he could have appeared at least as an influential Sadducee with a prominent place in the Sanhedrin in the holy city of Jerusalem. Instead, he came and lived as a carpenter in the small town of Nazareth—a place too insignificant to be mentioned either in the Old Testament or the writings of Josephus, the first-century Jewish historian."[9]

Jesus cannot be separated from his life. He suffers under the power of the legal and religious structures that enslave man. Therefore, he finds himself identified with the victims of these powers: the outcasts, the prostitutes, the helpless, the poor, the sick, the lepers, the sinners, etc. All of them were failures and defeated in their personal and social lives. Certainly, Jesus himself could not be considered a successful person.

Undoubtedly, these statements sound strange because we are not used to them. After all, our philosophy is also associated with the concept of victory. Based on this, it is not possible for the doctrine of the theology of prosperity to place the outcry of frustration and defeat on Jesus' lips. This rationale does not allow us to adopt the idea that in the very core of Christian faith we must hear a savior's outcry—Jesus—forsaken by God on the cross.

We might think that the outcry on the cross, in that it revealed weakness, could indicate that Jesus was not divine. In other words: would Jesus no longer be God's Son for having expressed pain and deep dissatisfaction for being abandoned? No. In spite of how terrible it sounds, Jesus' outcry

---

8. Ibid., 100.
9. Sider, *Rich Christians*, 51.

finds its logic in the disciples' experience of feeling Godforsaken; it is an outcry important to life itself, as it is the outcry that many humans—hurt, as Jesus himself was hurt—identify themselves with. Some of Moltmann's words help to illustrate this: "God is always on the side of the victims—indeed he himself is the victim in, with, and among the victims of those who wield power. This world's history of suffering is the history of God's suffering too, the God who does not merely permit the evil act because he wishes men and women to be free, but also endures the evil act in the victims, and receives only the victims into eternal community with him. A God who cannot feel suffering cannot understand us."[10]

The perverse logic of a McDonaldized theology keeps us from clearly seeing that the success of every society is measured by the living conditions of the poor and weak. At a minimum, it is the model for the biblical experience, which reminds us that in Israel kings were evaluated according to the way they defended the weak—widows, orphans, and foreigners—from the abuse of the rich. Otherwise the voice of the prophets was raised in protest. Consider, for instance, Amos who condemn the ruling elite of the northern kingdom of Israel because they enjoyed a life of material luxury but were not grieved by "the ruin of Joseph" (Amos 6:1–6). In this sense, we cannot forget to mention Yahweh, the God of Israel, who accepts no bribes and gives food to widows and orphans (Deut 10:16–19).

Because we live in a society where only the victors are rewarded and, as a result, are ranked as having more "goodness," the losers are forced to adopt the public scale of value, which is built on competition in the public market, and end up condemning themselves as failures. To the defeated, in Moltmann's words: "Less money, less value, less self-confidence. Here, the market society, which rewards only the competent performers and the successful, brings with it severe personal and family problems. It has done away with the old society based on rank, in which people found their identity through their birth, family, and nation; it now assesses only performance and its success."[11]

Often, people who belong to the category of "poor" must keep it a secret. In Brazilian cities, for instance, when the inhabitants of slums or districts with large populations of poor apply for a job, they often have to fake their home address; otherwise they are not hired due to their

---

10. Moltmann, *Quem é*, 66.
11. Moltamnn, *God for a Secular Society*, 163.

peripheral social status. So from the beginning, if the poor do not use deceit, they are condemned to unemployment. This is a completely dehumanizing scenario: the poor must deny even their social geography, their roots. Thus, not only does their subjectivity become a risk to them, but so too does their history and the group they belong to. In this case, the denial of their world becomes a ticket for them to enter another world, one that will never belong to them.

Therefore, it is necessary to change this perverse logic that condemns both the human being and God himself. When this logic is inverted, we begin to realize that where a child suffers the torment of hunger, God himself is tormented. Where a homeless man dies from the cold, God himself suffers the homeless man's death. "Though I make my bed in hell, you are there," says Ps 139 about the omnipresent God; even in the hell of hunger, failure, sickness, and suffering, God is there—not as the Lord of history, but as a victim among millions of victims.

THE SOCIAL PLACE OF GOD

How can we declare the victor's sovereignty in a society of the defeated? Theology is constantly presented as a gospel testimony and consequently a testimony of life. We cannot separate theology from life at the risk of condemning theology to be anti-theological. Without an eye for life, a testimony is nothing more than a vision; without sensitivity, a theologian is nothing more than a charlatan, and his theology, a pure illusion. Nevertheless, we keep looking for signs of the presence of God; and we search for them in our income, in our large "temples," in our relations with the prestigious, and in our statistics.

Kitamori's concern is fundamental when he proposes that God himself was shaken, hurt, and suffered for having embraced the ones who were not supposed to be embraced.[12] With such a viewpoint, it is completely obvious that a God who does not get involved in anything, who does not identify himself with anyone, is a God without pain. We can go so far as to say that the God who suffers is the only one who embraces the victims of history with solidarity. Alves adds: "The slave may forget about his suffering, but God does not. God is the suffering God, the God who does not ever allow the pains of history to be overlooked and healed by the hypnotic power of the politics of preservation . . . God is not the

---

12. Kitamori, *Teologia*, 23.

explanation of the pains of the world. On the contrary, he is the permanent power that denies the justice and right of suffering in history by being himself: the God who suffers."[13]

Hegel, however, has a different perspective when he claims that God does not suffer pain, in spite of embracing everyone. "He keeps going as a universal being, imperturbable, and invulnerable; a God who protects himself from any problem."[14] In this sense, Hegel's God is never able to suffer any wound. He is simply presented as a representation of the God who encompasses everything. Hegel's God cannot weep, for he has no tears. But a God who cannot suffer cannot love either; he is a loveless being. One is able to suffer because he is able to love and he always suffers only to the degree that he loves. If one kills all love in himself, he no longer suffers, but becomes apathetic.

So, I must agree with Moltmann when he argues, "A God who cannot suffer is poorer than any man. For a God who is incapable of suffering is a being who cannot be involved. Suffering and injustice do not affect him. And because he is so completely insensitive, he cannot be affected or shaken by anything."[15]

We face a divinity with abstract qualities from within extremely concrete situations. Certainly, this kind of representation ignores the fact that human history is marked by pain, suffering, poverty, and defeat. Any theology that fails in stating with absolute certainty the concept of God as one who embraces the victims of society, should abstain from making pronouncements on any other matter. Von Rad indicates that "even the earliest avowals to Yahweh were historically determined, that is, they connect the name of this God with some statement about an action in history."[16] Ergo, language about God (theology) is a language about events, their power, and their promise.

Justice and judgment are two key words in the Bible. The practice of both is one of the great biblical commandments (Gen 18:19), because they are tasks to which God is committed. However, justice and judgment cannot be promoted in the abstract but only in relation to the inhumane living situations of orphans, widows, and foreigners (remember that

13. Alves, *Theology*, 116–17.
14. Kitamori, *Teologia*, 33.
15. Moltmann, *Crucified God*, 222.
16. Von Rad, *Old Testament*, 121.

"orphans, widows, and foreigners" is a classic biblical synonym for "the poor").

The obligation of caring for the poor means that they are no longer people punished by God—as the theology of prosperity asserts—but rather friends of God. Thus, to give to the needy is to give to God: "He who is kind to the poor lends to the Lord" (Prov 19:17) and conversely, "He who oppresses a poor man insults his Maker" (Prov 14:31). The full implications of this attitude and the full extent of the obligation it imposes are revealed when Christ identifies himself with the poor of this world (Matt 25:31–46).

The language of the theology of prosperity doesn't even get close to the real God, who has a predilection for the poor precisely because divine love refuses to see the poor confined to the category of disposable. God has a preferential love for the poor not because they are necessarily better than others, morally or religiously, but simply because they are victims and live in an inhumane situation that is contrary to God's will.

A careful reading of Ps 22:7–9 and Pss 15–18 reveals a testimony of a man relating his disgrace and helplessness, but who, at no time, mentions his personal faults as the reason for his adversity. On the contrary, this person is an *innocent* man, treated unfairly. As with anyone plunged into inhumane conditions, he faces suffering and isolation, but he does not weaken. In his faith, he knows his God wants justice; God hears and protects him.

With liberation, God's action is manifested among the poor, the defeated, and the sick. We should not look for him anywhere else. Yahweh is the God of concrete historical events. Therefore, we should be attentive to what is happening around us. Otherwise, we run the risk of encountering an anti-theology, one with a doctrine that refuses to abandon history in the search for a meta-historical principle in which the contradictions of history are transcendentally reconciled.

We should not look for God's presence where he is not to be found, but where his presence is certain and his being-speaking-acting exercises its unique liberating power. Using Alves' terminology: "The biblical language about God is not descriptive of an ontology or metaphysics. It refers to what has happened, goes on, and can occur in history."[17]

---

17. Alves, *A gestação*, 90.

If we look in the Bible for an answer to the question "Who is God?," we will find it rooted in the history of a people, one which endures in our memory:

> A wandering Aramean was my father; he went down with a few people into Egypt and there he became a nation, great, mighty, and populous. But the Egyptians treated us harshly; they afflicted us. Then we cried to Yahweh, the God of our fathers, and Yahweh heard us, and saw our affliction, our toil, and oppression. And Yahweh brought us out of Egypt with mighty hand and outstretched arm, with great terror, with signs and wonders, and brought us to this place and gave us this land, a land flowing with milk and honey.
> (Deut 26:5–9)

The experience of exodus is the founding experience of biblical faith. Such an experience places us within a context where humanity was condemned to live on the fringes of life and, defeated, had no hope. For this reason, in the accounts of this experience, we find revelations of the cruel and doleful situation in which these enslaved people lived. People who grieve know that suffering is not God's ideal. Therefore, their grief expresses their aspiration for the plenitude of life.

Recall that in the religions of the ancient Near East, the rulers (such as the pharaohs) were considered "sons of God." In this context, when the slaves began to celebrate and recognize a liberating God using a new language, we realize that, in an opposing sense, the oppressors' gods were present as well. When the rulers invoked these gods, it was a reflection of their very existence as oppressors. It was in this ancient Near Eastern setting that gods such as Marduk from Babylon, Amon from Egypt, and many others were worshiped. They were considered gods who created and organized the cosmos, or the patrons of the ruling dynasty, as well as protectors of city-states that held the political hegemony. For Croatto, such gods are easily transformed into archetypes of the domination of one nation over another.[18]

Nevertheless, if the world is sacred and belongs to the gods (since they created it), human marginalization is unavoidable: the world has no place for men and women. Their destiny is to work for the gods. It is evident that the economies of the ancient Near East were centered in the temples, which included the kings' palaces. Humans were an economic

---

18. Croatto, "*Os ídolos*," 45.

necessity but nothing more. The gods, who were the legal landowners, had the king as their representative on earth and, because of that, he was divine. Consequently, everything related to divinity could be monopolized by the king.

This was a hidden way to justify the absolute power of the king. He could make use of the country's wealth, demand heavy tribute and taxes, or request workers for his needs. The exodus story can be seen as the history of an encounter. It shows the intrinsic relationship between a liberating God—who inserts himself into history—and people who live on the edges of history. God uses this historical event of pain and defeat to reveal himself and then to act. He manifests himself as an instrument of freedom. His manifestation is intentional and his presence is not a disinterested one. Yahweh is no longer in the heavens where those in the Old Testament—including Job's friends—believed he lived. Even today we should be aware that Yahweh's self-revelation in the history of the oppressed happened in the midst of a situation full of death. The slaves' freedom from Egypt originated within the heart of a considerate God. Therefore, theophany is the plan of a liberating God—Yahweh—emerging from outside of history, leading us to understand his domain over human history itself. The following passage exhibits God's multifaceted purpose:

> I have also heard the groaning of the Israelites whom the Egyptians are holding as slaves, and I have remembered my covenant with Abraham, Isaac, and Jacob . . . I will free you from the burdens of the Egyptians and deliver you from slavery to them. I will redeem you with an outstretched arm and with mighty acts of judgment. I will take you as my people, and I will be your God. You shall know that I am the Lord your God, who freed you from the burdens of the Egyptians.
>
> (Exod 6:5–7)

Yahweh's self-revelation becomes concrete and reveals God's desire to show his liberation in the history of people who suffer—people who are victimized by society. As Gustavo Gutierrez, argues, "Yahweh is a God who has acted since the reverse of history,"[19] or rather, he impossibly acts through those who have no ability to bring about history. He acts in

---

19. Gutierrez, *A força*, 328.

situations of death and oppression, in order to create a plan of social and political equality.

In an era when human life was highly devalued, Yahweh introduces himself as a God of solidarity. Then, a new story begins, or rather, a theology begins with the defeated, the oppressed, the marginalized. By revealing himself in the history of a people who lived in the periphery, Yahweh proposes life instead of death.

The history of humanity becomes the place of honor where Yahweh reveals his face. In their history, they experience an encounter with a God who lives with them and takes part in their struggle for freedom, who is committed to transforming the reality of the oppressed.

Yahweh's presence becomes the predominant characteristic of an imminent freedom. Something is about to happen. He manifests himself because he cannot be neutral as history unfolds. It is necessary for him to reveal himself, to side with the ones who suffer, who are defeated by society.

Starting with the understanding that God reveals himself in history, and for freedom, the question then becomes: Where can his presence be noticed today? Based on the above, we can suppose that it is in the periphery, because we believe that is the place in greatest need of abundant life; it is there that God reveals himself. God was and will always be the orphans' father, the widows' protector, supporter of the foreigner and offerer of relief for the oppressed. Going deeper, we can say that God is not exclusively in cathedrals, amid worshipers and choirs; but more often among the suffering. Karl Barth opines:

> God sides with the poor . . . In the Bible there isn't any passage where the right of the wealthy are proclaimed or where God appears as the Lord and savior of the wealthy and their wealth. On the contrary, there are passages where the rights of the poor are proclaimed. There aren't either passages where wealth is praised in any sense and where rich people are confirmed and exalted. On the contrary, the poor are promoted as fortunate and nominated as the elected of God and where the word "poor" is synonym of upright. That one the Bible calls God, sides with the poor.[20]

Thus, the poor and the defeated are the ones who have the privilege of being bestowed with God's grace and mercy, not the wealthy. While the

20. Barth, *Dádiva*, 352.

poor, with their lives marked by suffering, humbly open their hearts to receive support from their God and Father; the rich exude the arrogance produced by wealth.

For these reasons we are led to see that God's revelation has always occurred amid the starving, homeless, naked, and impoverished people. When we turn to the Bible, we see that the relationship between Yahweh and people can only be personal, for God is personal and communicates as such. His calling asks for a response, because Yahweh, through his action, wants to be involved in our history. He is not apathetic. If so, he would be cruel and distant. He cannot be compared to a cold and celestial power, isolated and detached from the world and human history. Moltmann, again, helps to illustrate this view:

> The prophets had no "idea" of God, but understood themselves and the people in the situation of God. Heschel called this situation of God the *pathos of God*. It has nothing to do with the irrational human emotions like desire, anger, anxiety, envy, or sympathy, but describes the way in which God is affected by events and human actions and suffering in history. They affect Him because He is interested in His creation; His people and His right . . . the history of God cannot therefore be separated from the history of His people. The history of the divine *pathos* is embedded in this history of men.[21]

Thus, we cannot identify God's *pathos* with his being, for even among the prophets it was not something concrete, but in the form of his relationship to others. The divine *pathos* is expressed in the relationship of God to his people. The concept of an apathetic God was inevitably alien to God's people in the Bible.

Yahweh's sympathy is revealed through his communication. Therefore we can say his nearness is experienced through his *pathos*, and his *pathos* is his love for freedom, his impassioned interest in life over death. He cares for the oppressed and the discriminated against because he suffers their pain and hears their anguished cries coming from the fringes.

What we have seen so far is simply the Almighty God, the Holy One, allowing himself to relate to his chosen people. And when he opens himself to them, everything changes. The divine begins to take part in human history. When he speaks, life and hope emerge from where they did not

21. Moltmann, *Crucified God*, 270.

previously exist. When he talks, he acts. His Word—and the theology built on it—is never theoretical, but is action on behalf of life.

In the exodus event, when we see God blessing human history by acting within it, we see a divine "unification" taking place. We could call this the action of a unifying God. This is the most likely reason for Yahweh's presence: to be one with those who live on the fringes. The circumstances of pain and defeat are where an experience of God is lived out. Where the poor, the oppressed, the small are; *there* God acts. Suffering is, thus, the element that establishes Yahweh's solidarity in relation to the oppressed.

God's action is a binomial composed of solidarity and pain; two processes in just one history. The greater the oppression and pain, the more Yahweh's presence is felt. The more pain, the greater the relationship between the liberators and liberated and the more a freer spirituality is lived out, as it emerges from within the context of a lifelong solidarity, breaking the ties of oppression for good. Therefore, we can say that God is present because he dwells among the victims and the sufferers, comforting them through his eternal companionship.

But we can also observe that God's sympathetic action provokes a response from his people. They abandon their lethargic state and open themselves up in solidarity to one another. Thus, the possibility of apathy and individualism in human relations is also broken. According to Moltmann:

> In the sphere of the apathetic God, man becomes a *homo apatheticus*. In the situation of the *pathos* of God he becomes a *homo sympatheticus*. The divine pathos is reflected in man's participation, his hopes, and his prayers. Sympathy is the openness of a person to the present of another. It has the structure of dialogue. In the *pathos* of God, man is filled with the Spirit of God. He becomes the friend of God, feels sympathy with God and for God. He suffers with God's suffering. He loves with God's love. He hopes with God's hope.[22]

Indeed, Yahweh is a God who places himself alongside human beings, amid their pain and the drama of struggling to survive amid unfair circumstances. He is extremely interested in their lives, in their development towards a worthy life. When God enters and takes part in the social aspects of the human life, he appropriates the lives and actions of those

---

22. Ibid., 272.

who live on the periphery as if they were his own. The words and actions of the oppressed become actions and words of God himself. They no longer belong to the oppressed. We should take it as a given: God embraces the oppressed. Yahweh takes on the human condition and opens a new future to the poor. God's companionship is the beginning and end of their freedom.

Such companionship is meant for the people. This lifelong joining is indicative of a practice of love and a commitment to justice not to the cultivation of privileges. According to Cesar, the Bible never speaks of freedom in the abstract.[23] Solidarity becomes real only through Yahweh's presence. This unity stood out in criticism of the religious system of the ancient Near East, whose gods defended an ideology of oppression; apathetic gods who did not interfere in the lives of the suffering. On the contrary, they legitimized the acts of governors and kings who acted against people's interest and on their own behalf; a religion for victors by victors!

Severino Croatto gives details about this victors' relation:

> Royalty was seen as the gods' gift. Thus, the king was the concessionary of the divine rights on earth. The king of a city-state and its tutelary god were structurally equivalent, though in different ways. Their functions were parallel. In both cases there is an accumulation of power that is gradually redistributed among the subordinates down to the slave. Since the order in force was accepted by tradition (thus, interjected) as a divine model, it was seen as perfect and eternal.[24]

It is clear that Yahweh joins with the slaves in Egypt against the gods who propagate death and against the Pharaoh's political system. This confrontation would become, in the history of the revolution of exodus, an expression of faith of an entire marginalized race. This idea is supported by the preamble to the Ten Commandments that begins with a reminder of this revolution. Before he hands down the two Tablets of the Law, Yahweh identifies himself: "I am the Lord your God, who brought you out of the land of Egypt, out of the house of slavery" (Deut 5:5; Exod 20:2). Yahweh is the one who frees from bondage. The God of the Bible desires to be known as the liberator of the defeated and oppressed.

---

23. Cesar, "*Violência*," 39.
24. Croatto, "*A dívida*," 55.

The experience recounted in the Book of Exodus shows us that the one force that comes from the periphery is the outcry. Specifically an outcry that stems from the breaking point of violence. This outcry is the moral awakening to the fact that these living conditions are unsatisfactory. On the contrary, the situation is one that transforms human beings into things until they are completely devalued. More powerfully, their outcry signals a desire for change. Thus, it is an outcry of revolt.

This outcry indicates that the victims are becoming aware of their situation, and have begun travelling the path towards freedom; when the victims cry out, they raise their voices and they cry out in protest and denunciation. It is a painful outcry that comes from the mouth of the oppressed. The outcry devolves into a moan simply because it has finally been laid bare, and expresses the pain that prevents human beings from assuming their true place in a world ruled by death.

There is one thing we must consider. Yahweh is affected by the outcry that comes from the lips of the victims of society. Consequently, his action begins from within history, since the victim's outcry comes from a historical, concrete, and identifiable situation. It affects the victims physically and emotionally; it involves them integrally. The pain that comes from such situations is very strong. It comes from deep within the bowels of life and requests an answer from those who hear it; a *praxis*. And so it happens: from their last bit of strength, the oppressed people create a powerful weapon—an outcry that is carried by the wind to the entire world and initiates a praxis from a God who embraces the ones who suffer and cry out. In the face of pain, Yahweh comes, assuming such pain and showing the way to liberation. When Yahweh places value on the victims of society he does not see them as objects, excluded and defeated, but as human beings who suffer.

Faced with the compassionate Yahweh's encounter with the outcry of a people marginalized in history, we reach the same conclusion as Tournier: "It is not possible to subtract God's humanity. If so, we would have but a glacial, remote, immutable God; a God strange to life, strange to history, strange to our own life; a god of philosophers and not the live God from the Scriptures. A God without feelings would be a God without soul, dead, even deader than Nietzche's God."[25]

---

25. Tournier, *Culpa*, 166.

Yahweh is thoroughly God because he is thoroughly marked by sympathy: He suffers to bring about a released and freed world. God himself has assumed the cause of the oppressed. Thus, God's participation in the suffering of humanity ends up impeding the rise of apathy and accommodation. At the same time, it helps to develop within people a sympathy for God and opens a path for God's hope for the future.

RELIGION AND MARKET

A market-driven society potentially produces a market-driven religion: society and religion exclude the great majority of those who see themselves as defeated and unable to take part in a society of consumerism. They are defeated but—as Job—do not remain silent. It is then that, because of the victims, the entire structure built by this market, and the social relationships it has spread and imposed, are questioned. Certainly, these are exploitive relationships that exclude the majority and produce death, by denying the victims the right to participate in a life for all. Such relationships are not based around human needs.

The laws of the marketplace, which must be fulfilled at all costs, include the laws of religion. As a result, they are considered God's laws. Therefore, any accomplishment must be approved by the marketplace. Life begins to be legitimized as "true" from the viewpoint of the marketplace. Outside the marketplace there is no life, and only consumerism offers the possibility of redemption. Therefore, the one who does not fit in is excluded. Lyon speaks of consumerism in similar terms, as being a kind of salvation: "Consumerism has become central to the social and cultural life of the technologically advanced societies in the later twentieth century. Meaning is sought as a 'redemptive gospel' in consumption. And cultural identities are formed through processes of selective consumption."[26]

The subject is excluded and sacrificed by the imposing of the laws of the market, and not simply because he is considered a sinner. In Hinkelammert's words, "the sacrificed subject is transformed in an individual who no longer knows salvation outside the market. Without value, the human being, as a subject, has rights nowhere only through and in the market . . . when he is a victim of the market, he is pronounced guilty."[27]

---

26. Lyon, *Pós-modernidade*, 74.
27. Hinkelammert, *Sacrifícios*, 158.

In the philosophy of market theology, there is no room for human freedom. Such freedom requires humanity, which is constantly denied by the market. By this logic, no victim can be autonomous. The victim that assumes autonomy is no longer a victim. Such a victim leaves the arena of exclusion and periphery and begins to acquire his own subjectivity, and so, starts to demand—what a blasphemy—to be called "human being." However, from the moment the victim starts demanding his humanity, the market is endangered to where it feels pressured and threatened.

The absolute and sacred market law leads to an idea of harmony and progress but without victims there is no economic progress. And, according to Hinkelammert, a subject searching for his own autonomy is "previous to the market and all the other institutions."[28] He is a subject with needs inherent to any human being and, for this reason, trying to satisfy his needs is a matter of humanity and social justice. When the market denies the satisfaction of the victim's needs, it also denies them legitimacy; they threaten it because they are grounded in realities that are prior to and stand outside of the market. At the same time, the market increases expectations that the consumer's desires *will* be satisfied, expectations that will never be met. A McDonaldized theology acts inhumanely. If human dignity is identified with market values, in Moltmann's words: "that dignity is enduringly destroyed, as the long-term unemployed discover for themselves, and as managers threatened by what they suppress learn from their psychiatrists. Human beings are more than the sum of their achievements, and more than the sum of their failures. Women and men must be respected as persons before God, and must be liberated from their market value—or non value."[29]

Any human struggle for emancipation is now seen, from the "godlike" perspective of the market, as though it was Lucifer wishing to be like God and, through this wish, becoming a demon. That's why every human attempt for emancipation may be called "Lucifer-like." Consequently, we find the absolutization of what is, in reality, social chaos presented in the guise of a natural element, essential to society. The market laws are considered to be part of the fabric of reality—they exist even "before the creation of the world."

---

28. Ibid., 159.
29. Moltmann, *God for a Secular Society*, 223.

So, the existence of progress is as natural as the existence of the victim. Victims are necessary for progress. The system of rules currently imposed on society favors progress and in such a system, everything that favors progress is good and necessary. However, it is important to notice that the quality of life that is improved is not that of the victims but of the ruling classes. The marketplace strictly controls the gates of progress. Only those who can afford it are the ones who can enter. As a result, the ruling classes are those who enjoy the new technologies and their impact. Comblin's intuition is correct when he claims, "The poor get very limited advantages. There is no evidence that the progress of sciences produces a [closing of the division] between the richer and the poorer. On the contrary, the result is a larger and increasing separation."[30]

We can best view the market and its makeup as an abstract institution and then establish the best way to analyze it. Obviously, the problem is not the market per se, but rather, its idolatrous claim to primacy and totality. A human being cannot be reduced to simply one who buys and sells. Profit at any cost and without consideration combined with uncontrolled consumerism physically kills those who do not have access to the system and morally kills those who are supposedly favored by it.

We know that technological progress along with capitalistic expansion demands a high social cost that, in religious terms, can be properly characterized as a "sacrifice" of human life. Such sacrificial violence of modernity is presented as a natural consequence for market "messianism" or idolatry. From this perspective, the sacrificial demands made on behalf of the market are irrefutable proofs of market "messianism."

All of these sacrifices end up legitimized by progress, or, rather, they create the myth that every sacrifice is rewarded with abundant life for all—in the future. Capitalism has created an environment in which all are theoretically free to buy and sell anything, even themselves. But if this freedom reduces everything to a commodity, at what point do we lose our very humanity? Theology has a responsibility to preserve a space in society in which people may be respected as their very selves, without regard to the part they play in the global economy. As creatures of God, we have an innate dignity, which the demands of global capitalism must recognize.

---

30. Comblin, *A força*, 357.

The marketplace is creating a new form of modern religion. We cannot help but say that it seems a fundamental corruption of theology. The capitalist mystic is revealed as a real religion and, as religion, it transforms sacrifice into an important element for enabling economic progress to reach its objectives. It is the philosophy of sacrifice that dominates, or even the philosophy of victimizer and victim. However, God hates evil economic structures and unjust legal systems because they destroy people by the hundreds, thousands, and millions. Nevertheless, the world makes room for only one of them—God or capitalism? The die is cast!

Julio de Santa Ana makes a pertinent point: "When Milton Friedman indicates that to obtain an appropriate index of economical growth it must be based on a necessary 'social cost,' he uses an economic and religious language that, in economic and religious terms, can be translated as 'sacrifices.'"[31] So, when neo-liberalism demands sacrifice, it confirms its religious nature. However, it is important to stress that the task of theology is to maintain human dignity in situations where it is in danger of being sacrificed.

The marketplace reinforces inequalities and thus, produces victims. It produces life for only a small number of nations. For the great majority of humanity it produces death and social destabilization in a kind of social and economic Darwinism. In a society in which consumers are cast as the driving force of economic prosperity, the poor are worthless as consumers. After all, the products displayed in shopping centers tempt them, but they have neither credit cards nor bank accounts. Keynes puts it simply, "Consumption is the sole end and object of all economic activity." Thinking of consumption on behalf of efficiency is idolatry. Sider shows us that theology needs to refute Keynes's words: consumption is *not* the sole end of economic life.[32] It is economy that is made for the people, not people for an autonomous, efficient, ever-expanding economy.

But we should not think that the poor are being reclassified by the consumer society as an inferior class. An even bigger deviation is coming. According to Bauman the poor start being "a class outside the classes, a category cast permanently off-limits from the 'social system,' a category the rest of us would be better off and more comfortable without."[33]

---

31. Santana, *O amor*, 60.
32. Sider, *Rich Christians*, 143.
33. Bauman, *Individualized Society*, 75.

We can see the Darwinism in a new theological system that selects who must and can continue living or surviving. But this is not the natural order of things, as Novak points out: "In democratic capitalism, inequalities of wealthy and power are not considered simple evils just for themselves, but are tuned with natural inequalities that everybody witnesses every day."[34] This thesis is repugnant precisely because it legitimizes a system without equal results, but with the impression of equal opportunities. For capitalism, the simple repression of human energy (which expresses inequalities and therefore is universal and perennial) creates an even greater evil.

It is critical to change the way this matter is seen. Such a change can be initiated simply with a set of questions, like those well posed by Moltmann. He says that, in a socially unstructured society, where the signs of misery are chronic and ubiquitous, the basic question to ask is: "Why does God permit this?" However, such a question stems from a distorted and unilateral view. It is an inquiry made by one who watches the death of his fellows passively, sorrowfully but passively. However, Moltmann proposes a new question; this one from the true outlook of the victims, which has a new point of view of reality: "Where is God?"[35] This is the question of a victim who tries to understand God from a place of non-victory. On the contrary, such an inquiry suggests the understanding of a new existential dimension, that is, the communion of God with the victim's suffering; a single communion among the victims produced by the same social environment of chaos and human degradation; where victims multiply; where victims grow poorer, and more and more numerous. The premise of the first question—the "why"—is that of an apathetic God who is supposed to justify himself before human suffering. The second question, the "where," seeks a God who shares our suffering and carries our grief.

If we allow the theological language about the real presence of God to run through these dimensions of misery, we reach, according to Moltmann, the following series of identifications:

> In the vicious circle of poverty it can be said: "God is not dead. He is bread." God is present as bread in that he is the unconditional, which draws near, in the present sense. In the vicious circle of force,

---

34. Novak, *O espírito*, 111.
35. Moltmann, *Quem é*, 33.

> God's presence is experienced as liberation for human dignity and responsibility. In the vicious circle of alienation, his presence is perceived in the experience of human identity and recognition. In the vicious circle of the destruction of nature, God is present in joy, in existence, and in peace between man and nature.[36]

We cannot know the exact number of people lacking even minimal nutrition, clothing, and shelter. The number varies depending on harvests, war, natural disasters, economic politics, etc. However, more than a billion desperate neighbors live in abject poverty and another two billion are poor. In spite of this, some Christian people, supported by their theological constructions, insist on claiming they are defeated, that they are not neighbors; and worse, that God is not with them.

JESUS AT MCDONALDS: EXCLUSION IN THE GLOBAL MARKET

The ethical guide that the theology of prosperity expounds is a simple one that can be applied in a highly individualistic way. It is a convenient and soothing theology for those who have great wealth. On the other hand, it promotes resignation and a sense of guilt in those who lack such wealth. Over the course of the history of the church certain movements in the Christian world have repeatedly breathed new life into this ethical doctrine. It regards wealth as God's reward to the honest and hard working, and poverty as God's punishment to the sinful and the lazy.

But we know the capitalist ideology has historically made use of this doctrinal expedient—openly in the beginning and nowadays in more subtle forms—for its own religious justification. This manipulation of theology distorts one area that continues to remain significant, despite all teaching to the contrary, namely: Christian faith necessarily entails a personal and social ethic.

It is fundamental to emphasize that human beings have never been so threatened in their survival as in recent decades. The question of poverty has been discussed many times in many places, but people still seem to be unaware of the breadth and magnitude of this problem. However, Landes, in his study *The Wealth and Poverty of Nations*, says, "The big challenge and threat is the gap in wealth and health that separates rich and poor," and he calls that gap "the greatest single problem and danger

---

36. Moltmann, *Crucified God*, 337–38.

facing the world of the Third Millennium."³⁷ In this regard, it is important to note the following facts:

    a. Sider notes that the World Bank estimates that 1.2 billion people live in crushing poverty—trying to survive on one dollar or less a day.³⁸ In addition to these 1.2 billion who live in almost absolute poverty, another 1.6 billion are very poor, living on two dollars or less a day. This means that just under a half of the world's people (2.8 billion) try to survive on two dollars a day or less; seventy percent of these are women and children;

    b. Bauman, quoting the report of the United Nations Development Program, says that while the global consumption of goods and services was twice as big in 1997 as in 1975 and had multiplied by a factor of six since 1950, 1 billion people cannot satisfy even their most basic needs.³⁹

    c. Among the 4.5 billion residents of developing countries, three in every five are deprived of access to basic infrastructure: a third have no access to drinking water, a quarter have no accommodation to speak of, and one-fifth have no use of sanitary and medical services.

    d. One in five children spends fewer than five years in any form of schooling.

    e. The three richest men on the globe have private assets bigger than the combined national product of the forty-eight poorest countries; the fortune of the fifteen richest persons exceeds the total domestic product of the whole of sub-Saharan Africa. Less than 4 percent of the personal wealth of the 225 richest people would suffice to offer all the poor of the world access to elementary medical and educational amenities, as well as adequate nutrition.

    f. According to the United Nations Human Development Report (2003), the richest 5 percent of the world's people receive 114 times as much income as the poorest 5 percent. In fact, "the

---

37. Landes, *The Wealth*, 39.
38. Sider, *Rich Christians*, 2.
39. Bauman, *Individualized Society*, 114.

richest 1 percent receives as much as the poorest 57 percent." A mere twenty-five million Americans (the richest twenty-five million) enjoy as much income as the poorest two billion people in the world combined.

g. This chasm widens year after year. In 1960, the one-fifth of the world's people living in the richest nations enjoyed an income thirty times that of the poorest one-fifth. By 1990, the rich were sixty times richer. And by 1997, it was seventy-four times.

h. The richest 20 percent of the world's population receive 86 percent of the world income while the poorest 20 percent get only 1.3 percent.

i. The poorest 20 percent of the world's people (just over one billion) possess 1 percent of the world's wealth. In fact, the poorest 60 percent possess only 6 percent of the world's wealth. The richest 20 percent possess 81 percent.

j. The poor are a larger and much more visible subsection of the Southern hemisphere. Today the wealthiest 20 percent of the world's population control sixty times the resources of the poorest 20 percent. This percentage has increased dramatically in the last forty years, from a time when the proportion was closer to two to one;

k. This distribution of wealth is immensely unjust, especially in the light of the fact that much of the poorest 20 percent does not have the resources to assure food or medicine to their children;

l. 1.75 billion lack safe drinking water;

m. 800 million go hungry every day.

An analysis of the data above shows that the philosophy of exclusion is prevalent. And the crowd of the helpless is increasingly being incorporated into this group of the excluded. So, one must agree: one of the most striking aspects of the global situation today is the dramatic distance between the rich and the poor. But, today, these differences do not correspond to the differences between the United States, Europe, and Japan, on one hand, and the rest of the world on the other. In every country of the world there are very wealthy people who invest their money in New York banks, or in those in Tokyo or Zurich, and who travel regularly to do their shopping and vacationing in Miami or Paris or Hong Kong. Wealthy elites in poor nations have more in common with the rich in high-income nations than with the poor in their own.

Douglas' analysis summarizes this situation very well: "In the McDonaldized world, those at the margins, those without power, suffer most, particularly indigenous peoples. It is they who lose their own ways of understanding God and the world, who lose their own means of production and sustenance. In the McDonaldized world the local, the vulnerable, the particular are always sacrificed to the interests and power of the global."[40]

The words from Kofi Annan's speech at the World Bank Conference in Toronto (June 22, 1988), should influence and affect our theology: "We are all here because we believe poverty to be intolerable in a world of plenty . . . So long as every fifth inhabitant of our planet lives in absolute poverty, there can be no real stability in the world." The concentration of the means of production and staples in the hands of a few, and the oppression and exploitation of the many, is a severe violation of human dignity. According to Moltmann, "a world-wide economic situation which allows millions of people to starve is unworthy of humanity, and in Christian terms it is a violation of God's honor and glory, which is present in all human beings, since they are the image of God."[41]

With such a theology, under these conditions, how can the poor be told that God loves them? No other conclusion is possible but that we live in an economic system that does not offer a place to all. In it, the great majority of humanity is excluded. Undoubtedly, neo-liberalism can be considered the biggest wall ever built to separate a minority of privileged from a majority of excluded. This majority, facing greater and greater exclusion, are aware they were not born to be miserable, starving or victims, yet this could be their ultimate destiny.

The poor enter into a historical and existential crisis—excluded from a society that rejects them and that no longer works for them, but without which there is no salvation. This is truly a social and theological crossroad! Such religious appropriation by the marketplace is, according to Father Beto, quite evident in shopping centers:

---

40. Stackhouse et al., *The Local Church*, 203.
41. Moltmann, *God for a Secular Society*, 128.

> Almost all of them are architecturally designed as stylized cathedrals. They are temples of the Market God. One does not enter into them in ordinary clothes but in their Sunday best. People walk through marbled cloisters hearing the post-modern Gregorian sound, that of elevator music. In there, everything evokes heaven: there are no beggars, juvenile delinquents, poverty, or misery. With a pious look, the consumer contemplates chapels that ostentatiously display the venerated objects of consumption in rich showcases, welcomed by beautiful priestesses. The one who can pay cash feels as though he is in heaven; the one who writes a check or uses credit, in purgatory; the one that has no money, in hell. Before leaving, everybody communes at the "Eucharistic" table of McDonalds.[42]

We know that any form of "absolutization" engenders new idols; idols that burden with a double demand: worship and sacrifices. Maybe this is the picture we draw of neo-liberalism; of a system that claims to be both unique and a master. Even more, it sees itself as fixed, as all gods do. And as a lord, it proposes to us to love the marketplace and give ourselves up to it. And this market-god demands deprivation, self-denial, and continuous resignation.

All systems that think of themselves as exclusive and unique are built on the principle of creating and maintaining themselves as producers of exclusion. Neo-liberalism—which can be compared to capitalism taken to its outer limits—supports profit for its own sake. So neo-liberal capitalism is constituted by a total and omnipotent market.

Lyon is very clear about it: "Only those who fail to consume, who are insufficiently integrated into the consumer market, need fear the old panoptical methods of surveillance and social control that once kept order in the factory and the street. If the new social management cannot seduce them, only then might it resort to repression."[43] It is a world with well defined limits: those who sacrifice and those who are sacrificed; the victimizers and the victims; the ones who possess and can live better and so can live inside the system and, on the other side, the ones who do not possess, are nothing, and consequently, are left behind. They are disposable pieces of a system that is both homicidal and suicidal, as we live in a disposable society, a consumer society that reduces everything to economic terms.

---

42. Beto, "*Religião de consumo*," 5.
43. Lyon, *Pós-modernidade*, 66.

Rolling the idea around, we might even realize that we are faced with a theology associated with consumerism. Thereby, the most important premise of this theology would be: "I buy, therefore I am." A commodity that would normally be an intermediary between people (person-commodity-person) becomes the principal goal (commodity-person-commodity). It leads many to take the best of the marketplace as the paradigm of the human being. When Moltmann analyzes the instruments that are a threat to life, he establishes "the global market of everything," including relationships, as one of these instruments. His words are enlightening:

> The global market of everything and every service is much more than pure economics. It has the all-embracing law of life. We have become customers and consumers, whatever else we may be. The market has become the philosophy of life, the world religion, and for some people even "the end of history." The marketing of everything destroys community at all levels, because people are weighed up only according to their market value. They are judged by what they can perform or by what they can afford.[44]

From this radical inversion, human relationships also fall into a new pattern. For example: if I travel to a friend's home by bus, my value is less than the one who got there by Mercedes. In this sense, it is not me, the human, who makes use of an object. It is the highly desired object that gives me value, by increasing my worth in the social marketplace.

Simon properly reminds us: "we are human beings, not human havings."[45] To confuse "having" with "being" is to worship the gift, rather than the giver. It is also to forget that God alone determines our worth; not our possessions nor what others think of us. Here, it is important to note that eight centuries before Christ there already existed a biting criticism of the fetish of commodity; and we can find it in the text of the prophet Isaiah. Consider:

> The carpenter measures with a line and makes an outline with a marker; he roughs it out with chisels and marks it with compasses. He shapes it in the form of man, of man in all his glory, that it may dwell in a shrine. He cut down cedars, or perhaps took a cypress or oak. He let it grow among the trees of the forest, or planted a pine, and the rain made it grow. It is man's fuel for burning; some of it he takes and warms himself, he kindles a fire and bakes bread.

---

44. Moltmann, *God for a Secular Society*, 153.
45. Simon, *How Much Is Enough?*, 64.

> But he also fashions a god and worships it; he makes an idol and bows down to it. Half of the wood he burns in the fire; over it he prepares his meal, he roasts his meat and eats his fill. He also warms himself and says, "Ah! I am warm; I see the fire." From the rest he makes a god, his idol; he bows down to it and worships. He prays to it and says, "Save me; you are my god."
>
> (Isa 44:13–17)

In this situation, little by little, humanity loses its space and its right to life. The more the marketplace is imposed on him, the less possible it is for the human being to survive. The more total and absolute the market is, the more life itself is made relative. We live in the era of globalization. The requirement for people to join the global market is the payment of a high social price. Ergo, the ones who cannot afford it are simply excluded. They are dispensable and do not count. They have no assured right to enjoy development. The inversion is complete: the value of objects is now related to our place in society and the world.

We should remember though: poverty, not wealth, is what is being globalized. Globalization motivated by competition for profit or advantage will only multiply the forces that produce poverty and injustice. We need a new global vision of our common humanity and our shared responsibility for life on this planet. Globalization has changed some of the fundamental assumptions about our local responsibility for good stewardship, the creation and distribution of wealth, and the claims of justice.

Bauman reminds us that, "the fast globalizing and increasingly exterritorial economy is known to produce the very deepening wealth-and-incomes gaps between the better off and the worse off sections of the world population, and inside every single society."[46] But we cannot celebrate life in one part of the world, while ignoring suffering in another. Our faith demands us to extend neighborly concern not only to our friends, but also to the stranger, the resident alien, and the foreigner. Globalization, however, has made us see as the stranger our next-door neighbors or our best friends and closest family members. But what does our theology offer us in response to our new situation?

A theology must be lived out not only when Christians must speak prophetically on occasion; not only when they must speak sagely on occasion, but also when they must speak *politically* on occasion, using policy

---

46. Bauman, *Individualized Society*, 114.

analysis and compromise to preserve or to accomplish some little good for those who are hurt. Theology must also be lived out to avert the great harm that pride and envy still cause in the world. Thus, in the global village, theology arises to struggle against the evils that threaten our embodied life and our common life. Liberation from violence, brutality and poverty, should remain the theme of every practical theology and every theological praxis.

A THEOLOGY OF DESIRE AND CONSUMPTION

In our late-modern or early-postmodern times, the economic sphere permeates all other spheres to the extent that virtually all parts of society are touched by economic concerns. The advertising and marketing industry has a significant influence at all levels of society. Marketers create tastes, desires, and perceptions in order to stimulate sales and to influence how people live. This kind of society has a profound impact on spirituality, on Christian practice as well as on the development of theology.

Considering that we truly live in an economics-saturated culture in which individuals act as spiritual shoppers and spiritual vendors, by offering greater and greater experiential highs, what effect does all this have on theology? Quite possibly this: theology, in the form of the prosperity gospel, assumes as its principal function the encouragement of consumerism as evidence of God's action in one's life.

Theologies that adopt a marketing approach treat believers as customers. The underlying assumption is that customers are never satisfied and are liable to take their business elsewhere. Satisfaction is an elusive target, constantly moving and taking on new forms. As a result, when theologies decide to adopt entertainment as their main focus, they create a continuous expectation and desire for more. Marketing is not neutral; it fosters human desire as much as it satiates it.

Instead of challenging the logic of the current economic system, which the kingdom does wonderfully, consumer theology blesses the economic rules and creates transitory surface-level Christians in the process.

It is important to point out that neo-liberal economic thought is founded on the concept of *desire*, not need. It is not the search for happiness that motivates consumption, but the possibility of beating a competitor. To a certain extent, in an era of excesses like the one in which we live, money no longer satisfies people. Franz Hinkelammert previously warned of this rationale, saying that, in this kind of neo-liberal economy "men are assumed to have no necessities, only tastes."[47]

Consumerism has become the social and cultural life of our societies. We may very well be witnessing the search for "a redeeming gospel" through consumerism. The discussion is no longer about the basic and daily needs for subsistence, but about subjective considerations. The search for a life of quality—which implies overcoming a life of deprivation and suffering—is reduced to a desire for possessing things and fulfilling the standards of consumerism, imposed by the marketplace and by society itself. In this regard, David Lyon, asserts:

> Television and consumption culture belong to the same class, although it is a common mistake to give a simple causal status to the first. Both have symbiotically grown since the World War II. As Baudrillard suggests, the postmodern separates from modern when the production demand—consumers' demand—becomes central. And TV has everything to do with the production of necessities and desires, the mobilization of desire and fantasy, and the politics of entertaining. The objects of consumption are, in fact, a system of signals that differentiates the population.[48]

Consumerism brings about a completely new social condition. What, then, are the possible consequences for people's lifestyles and for social values such as solidarity, identity, or hope? Could we be, in fact, immersed in a consumer-driven society where everything is exhibition and spectacle with the public image at the core? All surface and no depth.

Consumerism and consumption are basic postmodern themes. In them, we are what we consume, what we can buy. They represent a realm of fantasy and, consequently, one of exclusion. And they are closer than we might suppose: "Consumption now affects the ways in which people build up, and maintain, a sense of who they are, of who they wish to be"[49].

Along these lines, Jung Mo Sung says: "liberal economic theories and the production of private companies are thought of in terms of the satisfaction of consumers' desires . . . but these desires are also presented as necessities." [50] Confusion is created mainly because the concept of human needs is replaced. Necessities such as food, water, housing, and

47. Hinkelammert, *Crítica*, 63.
48. Lyon, *Pós-modernidade*, 88–89.
49. Lyon, *Jesus in Disneyland*, 74.
50. Sung, *Desejo*, 49.

health are no longer discussed or analyzed. An objective and concrete reality makes room for the production of unlimited desire.

As Bauman asserts, "the concept of 'need,' deemed by nineteenth century economists to be the very epitome of 'solidity'—inflexible, permanently circumscribed, and finite—was discarded and replaced for a time by desire, which was much more 'fluid' and expandable than need."[51] But, now, it is desire's turn to be discarded. A more powerful, and above all more versatile stimulant is needed to keep consumer demand on a level with the consumer offering. Harvey Ferguson suggests that consumerism in its present day is not founded upon the regulation of desire, but upon the liberation of wishful fantasies. So, "The notion of desire links consumption to self-expression, and to notions of taste and discrimination. The individual expresses himself or herself through their possessions. But for an advanced capitalist society, committed to the continuing expansion of production, this is a very limiting psychological framework, which ultimately gives way to a quite different psychic 'economy.' The wish replaces desire as the motivating force of consumption."[52]

Fantasy drives our choices in the supermarket and in the shopping mall. We fantasize about the images, associations, and status that have been linked to various products. Shopping is therefore an activity that is driven to some extent by a search for something that is beyond ourselves. Thus, these fantasies cannot be satisfied or met in the same way that need or desire can. Fantasies remain with us, pushing us to search for the next best thing. In this sense, a fantasy is non-referential, because we are unable to locate its true end or its fulfillment.

In fact, we face a perverse erosion of the practice of human and neighborly solidarity. After all, how can we share if we always want more? How can we share if our every desire has not yet been satiated, and the possibility to satiate them is remote?

In this sense, society is eternally dissatisfied. Such dissatisfaction extends to everyone, driving them onwards in a frantic race of consumerism. And consumer desire does not slow relative to the amount consumed: the more people have, the more they want and the less satisfied they are after acquiring the object of their desire.

51. Bauman, *Liquid Love*, 75.
52. Ibid., 75.

The consumer's behavior becomes the axle around which society revolves. The freedom to consume is intrinsically connected to the consumer market. New cars, new toys, new cosmetics, new shoes are offered each day. In this super-industrial society where we live, the number of choices is huge and increasing. When Ward describes the consumer society, he sums it up this way: "Consumer society is like a race where the finishing line is moving faster than the runners. Each of us is cast in a sea of choices where what is at stake is our ability to be competent, to make the right choice. Consuming therefore becomes a fluid environment where we never come to the end or reach our goal. Instead of an eventual finishing point, all that we have is the addictive behavior of seeking the right choices."[53]

During the transformation of desire into objects, the options are so many and so varied that the human being sees himself constantly changing his opinion, always moving towards a different option. Even the idea of "luxury" makes little sense, as the point is to make today's luxuries into tomorrow's necessities. As there is no norm against which to transform some wishes into needs and to show other wishes as "false needs," there is no benchmark against which one can measure a standard of conformity. Rubem Alves warns us about what he calls "possessing speed."[54] Such speed emerges out of a movement from the stability of traditional societies to the transitory structure of a new society. In this case, the products of consumer desire are designed and built so that they do not last long or soon become obsolete.

We live amidst a restless society. It brings to mind a curious passage of Lewis Carroll in which he shows speed marking relationships:

> They were running hand in hand, and the Queen went so fast that Alice could not keep up with her: and still the Queen kept crying "Faster! Faster!" . . . The most curious part of the thing was that . . . however fast they went, they never seemed to pass anything . . . "In our country," said Alice, "you'd generally get to somewhere else if you ran very fast for a long time as we've been doing." The Queen said: "Now, here, you see, it takes all the running you can do, to keep in the same place. If you want to get somewhere else, you must run at least twice as fast as that.[55]

---

53. Ward, *Liquid Church*, 58.
54. Alves, *A gestação*, 46.
55. Rasmussen and Birch, *Prediment*, 88.

For Alves "the planned depreciation will reach all sectors of human life. The stability of objects will be extinguished: they soon will stop being enjoyable things in our hands, and then we will have to look for new ones."[56] Charles Kettering, director of the research division of General Motors, decided that the business needed to create a "dissatisfied consumer." So, the annual model change—planned obsolescence—was his solution. Success came to depend on the virtue of qualities like wastefulness, self-indulgence, and artificial obsolescence. As David Lyon properly warns, this brings serious social consequences: "At a social level, the pressure to spend comes from a symbolic rivalry and from the necessity to build our self [image], by acquiring what is distinct, different . . . Capitalism not only seems intact, but is even stronger, and can visualize a better future."[57]

It can be said that consumerism does not know any limits. In a society of consumers the sky is the limit. Undoubtedly, such a society would lead humanity to face a life ruled by endless options and disposable things. Something very similar to the society of Huxley's *Brave New World:* "Throwing away is better than fixing. The more you fix, the less you enrich."[58] The postmodern man's search for something new and exciting is insatiable. He is never satisfied with what he already possesses or experiences; therefore, he sets off on a search for a new experience, a new product. As we said before, products no longer last as long as they used to, and it is easy to see. Each new commercial cycle is shorter and shorter. In the kingdom of the disposable, the concept of "time" is constantly redefined such that consumers are "forced" to continuously search for a new product or model, even when the one they possess is not "old." In a consumerist society, the young is born old! Bauman is clear when he writes:

> Gratification and the obsoleteness are instant. Not just the contents of the wardrobe need to be changed every season—cars need to be replaced because their body design has become old-fashioned and hurts the eye, good computers are thrown on the scrap head because new gadgets have made them out-of-date, splendid and cherished music collections on long-playing records are replaced

---

56. Alves, *A gestação*, 46.
57. Lyon, *Jesus in Disneyland*, 101.
58. Huxley, *Admirável*, 78.

by cassettes only to be replaced again by CDs simply because new recordings are no longer available in previous forms.[59]

Sharing is replaced by selfishness. That is to say that such a society cannot work if all its members constantly act with benevolent intentions. The human being sees himself in-between the instantaneous and the ephemeral where his only interest is his own pleasure. Since the postmodern person has lost confidence in programs designed to transform society, his strengths are refocused on his personal achievements. The individual and subjective sphere of his life guides his search for accomplishment and happiness. Our individualistic heritage has taught us that there is no such thing as the common good but only the sum of individual goods. However, in our globalized and interdependent world, the sum of individual goods, organized only by the tyranny of the market, often produces a common evil that eventually erodes our personal satisfactions as well.

In this sense, theology is no longer understood as an instrument for an individual to reach self-fulfillment. Instead, theology becomes an instrument through which one enters the marketplace, feels fulfilled, and finally gets his certificate of "being human." Theology begins to be seen as the fuel that feeds the fire of desire.

The word "selfish" starts a process of semantic redefining. It is no longer linked to covetousness or to the anxiety of possession. On the contrary, it starts to codify a vision of human freedom that far exceeds individual interest. After this semantic doctoring, selfishness becomes a virtue. Consumerism destroys a community by discouraging active participation. Nevertheless, this poses a contradiction: where do I feel personally free: in a supermarket, where no one knows me but I can buy what I want as much as I can afford; or in a community where others accept me just as I am? A community in solidarity is a resistance against the domination and control of the society of the affluent.

We are faced with a process that takes what was once evil, and transforms it into a virtue, a virtue to be cultivated. Milton Friedman defines selfishness/virtue by the way a person's freedom of choice occurs according to his own self-interest.[60] In Friedman's vision, human beings always maximize their self-interest; and the primary measure of self-interest is

---

59. Bauman, *Individualized Society*, 156.
60. Santana, *O amor*, 67.

money. Consequently, economics becomes a comprehensive science that explains everything. As a result, economics has been censured under the allegation that it draws conclusions that are too general, based on a completely unrealistic "economic man," seeing him as a mere calculating machine that reacts only to monetary stimulation. For Friedman, this common concern about the market economy has given rise to a narrow interpretation that sees selfishness as an "exclusive concern about material rewarding" or as a "shortsighted self-esteem." In defense of this new semantic understanding, he asserts: "Selfish is not shortsighted self-esteem. It is anything that interests the participants, no matter their value, no matter the goals they seek: the scientist aims to surpass the boundaries of his subject, the missionary aims to convert the unfaithful into the real faith, the philanthropic aims to give comfort to the need—all seeking their interests in the way they see them, at the light of their own values."[61]

Mike Featherstone offers some reflections on a consumer culture. He identifies three perspectives on it:[62]

- consumer culture arises from the expansion of capitalist commodity production with its vast accumulation of material culture, both in goods for purchase and sites for consuming;

- we should look at how people consume, and consider what this says about their ways of creating social bonds or distinctions. In this case, satisfaction and status depend upon how goods and even images can be used to display and sustain differences between people;

- we should look at the pleasures it brings, and at the dreams and desires celebrated within consumer cultural imagery. And his conclusion is that, "social groups seek to classify and order their social circumstances and use cultural goods as a means of demarcation, as communicators which establish boundaries between some people and build bridges with others."

The postmodern individual seeks simple happiness based on hedonism and, consequently, on consumerism. For Hong, "The postmodern individual does not appear as a producer but as a consumer of the products

---

61. Novak, *Espírito*, 109.
62. *Featherstone, Consumer Culture*, 78.

offered by the market."⁶³ Such endless searching for happiness founded on consumerism converts the human into a being filled by a compulsive necessity to consume; someone who seeks newer, finer, and more stimulating products. Certainly that is the reason why advertising agencies use the most sophisticated combinations of beautiful women, gorgeous color, and splendid soundtracks to guarantee that self-indulgence and instant gratification replace frugality and simplicity. Lyon's description of this is fitting: "The popular image of the postmodern is of people flitting like butterflies from store to store and from symbol to symbol, constantly constructing themselves, trying on this fashion, that lifestyle. A sort of pastiche persona results, so the self—and life itself—becomes transient, ephemeral, episodic and apparently insignificant."⁶⁴

We could say that this scenario is that of wild, consumer-driven globalization. However, an exception must be made: consumerism is global not in the sense that everyone can afford to consume, but in the sense that everyone is affected by it, through integration or exclusion. And the ones excluded are the ones who do not consume. The question is: why should those who cannot afford to consume be excluded from simple participation in society, and therefore, simply stop being considered as citizens?

In this "tentacled" expansion, not even religion remains unscathed. No sphere is immune to the pressure of the marketplace. Consumer choice pervades the religious life, church life, and its theology. In this regard, Reginaldo Bibby argues: "religion became a delicately wrapped consuming item—assuming its place among other commodities that can be purchased according to everyone's whim."⁶⁵ The church runs a serious risk of losing its character, its identity as a "peculiar people" distinct from other organizations of society. It is an ill-informed, church—one that has lost its soul—that is convinced that material goods are the supreme value of existence. An irrelevant society leads an irrelevant church with an irrelevant theology.

Capitalism is an economic system centered around consumers' desires; an insatiable desire that touches everyone indistinctly. And, in this endless race towards an infinite consumerism that seeks to definitively satisfy every kind of desire, capitalism emerges in the guise of theology:

63. Hong, *Una iglesia*, 7.
64. Lyon, *Jesus in Disneyland*, 92.
65. Lyon, *Pós-modernidade*, 95.

God will most certainly satisfy the desires of all his believers, since they are not in sin. Note clearly the relationship between religious feeling and the marketplace. Religious feeling is used in areas usually reserved for the marketplace, in which one seeks profit. The use of a religious representation in order to gain simple economic objectives is very relevant in a society where competition becomes stiffer and stiffer and, consequently, the growth and amassing of capital becomes more difficult to achieve. Because theology tends to conform to the surrounding contemporary culture, it has appropriated values and customs that are more befitting the marketplace. As on a supermarket shelf, everything becomes fragmented, scattered, and plural, subjected to consumers' choice and preference.

A theology that encourages consumption becomes a focus of conflict because it divides human relations more than it unifies them, watering down (eroding away?) their objective of promoting cooperation and solidarity. In a wealthy society, encouraging improper behavior in relation to the poor shakes the foundations and connections of said society and provokes a risk of fragmentation. This standard is typical of a theology with a capitalistic mentality, which sells products, ideas, and lifestyles within the church. At the root of this experience is the tyranny of the hedonistic culture. In this sort of theology, the voice of consumerism is the voice of God. Growing up in this culture is listening to the voice of this god.

Consequently, it is not surprising that banal worship and banal literature have spread, creating a superficial theology, a consumer theology, which has no demands but only offerings. Why not go so far as to say that this hybrid theology is synthetic, artificial, and disposable? Why not say it has an irrelevant doctrine, considering that it is concerned with market research and adapts its message to listeners' necessities? The following was taken from a newspaper from the San Francisco Bay area: "the members of Saint John's Lutheran Church have a money-back guarantee. They can donate to the church for 90 days; then, if they think they made a mistake, or did not receive a blessing, they can have their money back. The program is called 'God's Guarantee' and the pastor is confident it will work—'we trust God to keep His promises, so much that we are offering this money-back policy,' he says."

Let us pose an old question in current terms: does the market exist for the sake of men and women, or do men and women exist for the sake of the market? Moltmann provides a possible answer for this question: "in families, neighborhoods and free communities, human relationships exist in mutual recognition and acceptance. If the market becomes the dominant power, then relationships of mutual recognition and acceptance come to an end."[66]

---

66. Moltmann, *God for a Secular Society*, 162.

Conclusion

A QUESTION WAS ON my mind throughout the course of this book. Maybe its answer can lead us back to better theological paths and ecclesial practices. This question could be formulated as follows: *More possession or more solidarity?*

The alternative to poverty is not possession, but the practice of solidarity. Human beings are not simply autonomous, competitive, consumerist, self-centered subjects, but rather, beings-in-community. The market economy promotes not only strong individuals but also weak communities, undermining the structures of solidarity and fracturing local communities. Consequently, any sort of theology that—in its incestuous relation with capital and profit—defends the paradigm of economic globalization that sees the human being as an economic being (*homo economicus*), should be unhesitatingly rejected.

The call for economic justice is a biblical imperative. But, some theologies can immediately lead us into a conflict zone with forces that deny people their basic human dignity. But just one scene helps us to understand this situation. It's the scene of the man with a "withered hand" (Mark 3), which happens in a synagogue on a "Sabbath." Everyone is looking at Jesus—among them many kinds of unsuccessful people—and his opponents are looking for a reason to accuse him. Note that Jesus is dealing here not only with religious authority but also with political power, as, under the terms of the Roman occupation, the Sanhedrin administered Jewish affairs. Nevertheless, Jesus continues his performance and heals the poor and sick man. In doing so, Jesus asks a simple question that confronts the religious and political powers and, at the same time, creates a new theology or, at least, shows what the prime task of theology is: "Which is lawful on the Sabbath: to do good or to do evil, to save life or to kill?"

It is clear in this narrative that the act of healing is not the central one. Jesus deliberately chose to confront an unjust, oppressive theology that put man's religious rules before people and denied the very character of God. But to do it, Jesus put his life on the line.

The world will change when we, as Christians, really obey the one we worship. And "to obey" means "to follow." Following Jesus' steps means having simpler personal lifestyles; it means transformed churches with a theology that worships the God of the poor, the defeated, and the oppressed; a theology that follows his steps among such discarded people, seeking for justice to relieve their agony, with the objective of building societal systems that work fairly for all.

Maybe we can counterbalance the theology of prosperity with the theology of "enough." The latter has a task of supporting the people to develop models of simpler lifestyles and practices that discourage overconsumption. Unlimited economic growth is an economic Tower of Babel, not a biblical goal.

For many years, the theology of prosperity has looked at the gospel and history from a superior position. The result is not a church for the poor, but a church of Christians that just looks at the poor from its own privileged position of wealth. Why? Because the presence of the poor denies God's presence and his victory. Probably, the poor are marginalized, pushed to the periphery, because they represent what people most fear and deny in themselves. If we are defined by how good we are feeling or how successful we are, that, also, is a fragile definition of success. We will always be up and down. It is the shallowness of a consumer culture opposed to an authentic religious culture.

A church that defends the theology of prosperity has become a middle-class and even upper middle-class church that largely avoids the Jesus of the Gospels, who preached against the rich and their wealth. Such a church sees no problem in doing so, as a lot of Christians today see no problem in being fabulously wealthy and still believe that they trust in God. They do not even read the Gospels correctly any more. If some passages do not fit in with their culture and lifestyle, they simply dismiss them.

Sometimes our theology saves us from our fear of failure, of being a refugee, or of not having a home or food, etc. Theology consumers promote self-interested exchange and this violates an inherent part of the gospel: the one that talks about the gift. Cecil is clear about this: "It is our conviction that one of the reasons Christianity is so consumerist is that we have prioritized the individual and have 'commodified' God. The church must share some responsibility for this monster we have created. We have made Jesus out to be the ultimate consumer commodity. He is packaged in a convenient needs-driven format of the one-hour God experience that happens every Sunday morning."[1]

It seems to me that God is asking us to save the church and its theology from any further distortion of the gospel. He is asking us to be in solidarity with weakness and the truth, to surround ourselves with those sacraments of brokenness. This way, we will have the courage to discover that we are also broken. The broken ones are no different than we are; they are only more visible sacraments of what we are trying to hide.

God is present among suffering people throughout the biblical narrative and he also suffers. Through his solidarity with the broken he declares the inhumanity and the falseness of the powers that dominate the current society. If we claimed here that God does not suffer, we would make God a demon. If we spoke here about an absolute God, it would make God an annihilating nothingness. If we spoke here about an indifferent God, it would condemn men to indifference.

In the first century, Jesus faced the exclusion of Palestine and confronted it with an *inclusive* community. The exclusivity of post-modernity, with its pursuit of "the same" and the exclusion of "the other," needs to be similarly challenged. Any social entity within post-modernity that aims to model the kingdom of God must confront the ordering and controlling aspects of our current context.

However, while in the first century, exclusion was a proposal coming from the outside to inside—that is, from society to church; today, exclusion is a proposal that emerges *from within the church itself.*

Theology cannot and ought not simply to exist for itself, not even become a chaplaincy for the affluent culture. On the contrary, theology must demonstrate an alternative society. It must seek to transform the world.

I think the best theological language is that one which is not connected to the free market. There are other theological languages that need to be heard and to be heard together, such as those of human dignity, the integrity of creation, justice, and peace. So I ask, "Market value or human

---

1. Gibbs and Bolger, *Emerging Churches*, 139.

dignity? What society do we really want?" The answer for this question also warns about the kind of theology that is being offered to believers and society.

Victory and success are beyond the narrow limits of any confession of faith. Consequently, being a Christian is not a guarantee of success in the same way that being wealthy is not a guarantee of happiness. Commitment to the biblical God frees us from the supposition that life can find its end and meaning in wealth and consumption. So, we see the quest for material goods as what it really is: a terrible form of idolatry that destroys our spiritual life, the human community, and even nature.

We conclude with a little poem from Michel Quoist (1921–97), for it reminds me that our God suffers; since a god that cannot feel pain, cannot understand the suffering of the ones who live on the periphery of society. This poem should be used as a compass to orient any theological labor:

> I am not made of plaster, God says, nor of stone, nor of bronze.
> I am living flesh, throbbing, suffering.
> I am among men, and they have not recognized me.
> I am poorly paid, I am unemployed, I live in a slum, I have tuberculosis, I sleep under bridges, I am patronized.
> And yet I said to them: "Whatever you do to them, however humble, you do to me." That's clear.
> The terrible thing is that they know it, but that they don't take it seriously. "They have broken my heart," God says . . .[2]

---

2. Quoist, *Prayers*, 7–8.

Bibliography

Ahlstrom, G. W. *The History of Ancient Palestine*. Minneapolis: Fortress, 1983.
Alcorn, R. *Money, Possessions and Eternity*. Chicago: Tyndale, 1989.
Alves, Rubem. A. *A Theology of Human Hope*. New York: Corpus, 1969.
———. *A Gestação do Futuro*. Campinas, Brazil: Papirus, 1986.
Ana, João. S. *O Amor e as Paixões*. São Paulo: Santuário, 1989.
Assmann, Hugo., and F. Hinkelammert. *A Idolatria do Mercado*. Petrópolis, Brazil: Vozes, 1989.
Barth, Karl. *Dádiva e Louvor*. São Leopoldo, Brazil: Sinodal, 1986.
Bauman, Zigmunt. *The Individualized Society*. Oxford: Blackwell, 2001.
———. *Liquid Love*. Oxford: Blackwell, 2003.
———. *Liquid Modernity*. Oxford: Blackwell, 2000.
Beto, Frei. "Religião do Consumo." *Jornal Ciência e Fé* 2.29 (April 2001) 23.
Bobsin, Oneide. *Desafios urbanos à Igreja*. São Leopoldo, Brazil: Sinodal, 1995.
Bonhoeffer, Dietrich. *Letters and Papers from Prison*. London: Bethge, 1971.
Briant, P. *From Cyrus to Alexander: A History of the Persian Empire*. Winona Lake, IN: Eisenbrauns, 2002.
Bright, John. *História de Israel*. São Paulo: Paulus, 2004.
Campos, Leonildo Silveira. *Teatro, Templo e Mercado: organização e marketing de um empreendimento pentecostal*. São Paulo: UMESP, 1999.
———. "Why Historic Churches are Declining and Pentecostal Churches are Growing in Brazil: A Sociological Perspective". In *In the Power of the Spirit*, edited by Dennis A. Smith and B. F. Gutierrez, 66–77 Drexell Hill, PA: Aipral/Celep, 1996.
Carter, C. E. "Syria-Palestine in the Persian Period." In *Near Eastern Archaeology*, edited by Suzanne Richard, 101–14. Winona Lake, IN: Eisenbrauns, 2003.
Castells, Manuel. *A questão Urbana*. São Paulo: Paz e Terra, 1983.
Cazelles, Henri. *História política de Israel*. São Paulo: Paulinas, 1986.
Comblin, José. *A Força da Palavra*. Petrópolis, Brazil: Vozes, 1986.
———. *Pastoral Urbana*. Petrópolis, Brazil: Vozes, 1999.
———. *Teologia da cidade*. São Paulo: Paulinas, 1999.
Connor, E. *Search for Silence*. San Diego: Luramedia, 1986.
Copeland, Kenneth. *The Force of Faith*. Fort Worth, TX: KCM, 1983.
———. *The Power of the Tongue*. Fort Worth, TX: KCM, 1980.
———. *Welcome to the Family*. Fortworth, TX: KCM, 1979.
Croatto, José. S. "A dívida na reforma social de Neemias—um estudo de Neemias." In *Revista de Interpretação Bíblica Latino Americana* 5-6 (1990) 25–34.

———. "Os ídolos da Opressão e a Busca de um Deus Libertador". In A Luta dos deuses, 33–45. São Paulo: Paulinas, 1985.
Dictionary of Christianity in America. Edited by Daniel G. Reid et al. Downers Grove, IL: InterVarsity, 1990.
Dandamaev, M. A. *A Political History of the Achaemenid Empire.* Leiden: Brill, 1989.
Dhorme, Edouard. *Le livre de Job.* Paria: Gabalda, 1926.
Donner, Hebert. *História de Israel e dos Povos Vizinhos.* Petrópolis, Brazil: Vozes, 1997.
Drane, John. *The McDonaldization of the Church.* London: Darton, Longamn and Todd, 2000.
Featherstone, M. *Consumer Culture and Postmodernism.* London: Sage, 1991.
Fee, Gordon. *The Disease of the Health and Wealth Gospels.* Beverly, MA: Frontline, 1985.
Foucault, Michel. *Em Defesa da Sociedade.* São Paulo: Fontes, 2002.
———. *Microfísica do Poder.* Rio de Janeiro: Graal, 1990.
———. *Vigiar e Punir.* Petrópolis, Brazil: Vozes, 1991.
Freire, Paulo. *Conscientizacion.* Bogotá: APE, 1972.
———. *La Educacion como Práctica de la Liberdad.* Montevideo, Uruguay: Tierra Nova, 1969.
———. *Pedagogia do Oprimido.* São Paulo: Paz e Terra, 1988.
Freston, Paul. "Visão Histórica". In *Nem Anjos nem Demônios,* edited by Alberto Antoniazzi, 67–159. Petrópolis, Brazil: Vozes, 1994.
Fromm, Erich. *El Corazón del Hombre, Breviario.* México: F.C.E., 1967.
Gelin, A. The Poor of Yahweh. Collegeville, PA: Liturgical, 1964.
Gerstenberger, Ehrard. *Leviticus.* Louisville: Westminster John Knox, 1996.
Gibbs, Eddie, and Ryan Bolger. *Emerging Churches: Creating Christian Community in Postmodern Cultures.* Grand Rapids: Baker Academic, 2005.
Gottwald, Norman K. *Introdução Sócioliterária à Bíblia Hebraica.* São Paulo: Paulinas, 1988.
Gutierrez, Gustavo. *Falar de Deus a partir do sofrimento do inocente.* Petrópolis, Brazil: Vozes, 1986.
———. *A Força Histórica dos Pobres.* Petrópolis, Brazil: Vozes, 1984.
Habel, Norman C. *The Book of Job.* London: Oxford, 1985.
Hagin, Kenneth. *How God Taught Me about Prosperity.* Tulsa, OK: Kenneth Hagin Ministries, 1985.
———. *I Believe in Visions.* Old Tappan, NJ: Revell, 1972.
———. New Thresholds of Faith. Tulsa, OM: Kenneth Hagin Ministries, 1972.
———. *Real Faith.* Tulsa, OK: Kenneth Hagin Ministries, 1979.
———. *Right and Wrong Thinking for Christians.* Tulsa, OK: Kenneth Hagin Ministries, 1966.
———. *Zoe: The God-Kind of Life.* Tulsa, OK: Kenneth Hagin Ministries, 1989.
Hanks, T. *God so Loved the Third World.* Maryknoll, NY: Orbis, 1983.
Hayes, H., and Miller, J.M. *Israelite and Judaean History.* Philadelphia: Trinity, 1990.
Hinkelammert, Franz. *Crítica da Razão Utópica.* São Paulo: Paulinas, 1986.
———. *Sacrifícios Humanos e Sociedade Ocidental: Lúcifer e a Besta.* São Paulo: Paulus, 1995.
Hobbes, Thomas. *Coleção Os Pensadores.* São Paulo: Nova Cultural, 1987.
Hoglund, K. G. *Achaemenid Imperial Administration in Syria-Palestine and the Missions of Ezra and Nehemiah.* SBLD 125. Atlanta: Scholars, 1992.
Hong, I. S. *Una Iglesia Posmoderna?* Buenos Aires: Kairos, 2001.

Huxley, Aldous. *Admirável Mundo Novo*. Rio de Janeiro: Bradil-Dinal, 1969.
Irvine, G. *Best Things in the Worst Times*. Wilsonville: BookPaterns, 1996.
Josefo, Flavio. *Las Guerras de los Judios*. Tomo I, Barcelona: Clie, 1998.
Kippenberg, H. G. *Religião e Formação de Classes na Antiga Judéia*. São Paulo: Paulinas, 1988.
Kitamori, S. *Teologia de la Dolor de Dios*. Salamanca: Sígueme, 1986.
Kushner, S. *When Bad Things Happen to Good People*. Pan, 1982.
Landes, D. S. *The Wealth and Poverty of Nations*. New York: Norton, 1998.
Leith, M. J. W. "Israel among the Nations: The Persian Period". In *The Oxford History of the Biblical World*, edited by Michael A. Coogan, 276–316. Oxford: Oxford University Press, 2002.
Libânio, João Batista, and A. Murad. *Introdução à Teologia*. São Paulo: Loyola, 1996.
Lyon, David. *Jesus in Disneyland: Religion in Postmodern Times*. Oxford: Blackwell, 2001.
———. *Pós Modernidade*. São Paulo: Paulus, 1998.
Macedo, Edir *Vida com Abundância*. Rio de Janeiro: Gráfica Universal, 1973.
Mariano, Ricardo. *Neopentecostais: sociologia do novo pentecostalismo brasileiro*. São Paulo: Loyola, 1999.
Mariz, C. L. "Pentecostalism and Confrontation with Poverty in Brazil". In *In the Power of the Spirit*, edited by Dennis A. Smith and B. F. Gutierrez, 31–47. Drexel Hill, PA: Aipral/Celep, 1996.
Metzger, M. *História de Israel*. São Leopoldo: Sinodal, 1981.
Miranda, J. *Carisma, Sociedade e Política*. Rio de Janeiro: Relume Dumará, 1999.
Moltmann, Jürgen. *The Crucified God*. Minneapolis: Fortress, 1990.
———. *God for a Secular Society: The Public Relevance of Theology*. Minneapolis: Fortress, 1999.
———. *Quem é Jesus Cristo para nós Hoje?* Petrópolis, Brazil: Vozes, 1997.
Monteiro, Douglas Teixeira. "Igrejas, Seitas e Agências: Aspectos de um Ecumenismo Popular". In *A Cultura do Povo*, edited by Edênio Valle, 123–34. São Paulo: Cortez & Moraes, 1979.
Novak, Michel. *O Espírito do Capitalismo Democrático*. Rio de Janeiro: Nórdica, n.d.
Orlandi, E. P. *Palavra, Fé e Poder*. São Paulo: Pontes, 1987.
Pixley, Jorge. *História de Israel a partir dos Pobres*. Petrópolis, Brazil: Vozes, 1989.
Preisswerk, Matthias. *Educacion Popular y Teologia de la Liberacion*. San José: ASODEI, 2005.
Proença, Wander Lara. *Magia, Prosperidade e Messianismo: o "sagrado selvagem" nas representações e práticas de leitura do pentecostalismo brasileiro*. Curitiba, Brazil: Quatro Ventos, 2003.
Quoist, Michael. *Prayers*. Lanham, MD: Sheed & Ward, 1963.
Rad, Gehard von. *Old Testament Theology*. New York: Harper & Row, 1967.
Rasmanussen, L. L. *The Predicament of the Prosperous*. Philadelphia: Westminster, 1978.
Ritzer, G. *The McDonaldization of Society: An Investigation into the Changing Character of Contemporary Social Life*. Thousand Oaks, CA: Pine Forge, 1993.
———. *McDonaldization: The Reader*. Thousand Oaks, CA: Pine Forge, 2002.
Rohr, Richard. *Job and the Mystery of Suffering*. New York: Crossroad, 1996.
Rossi, Luiz Alexandre Solano. *A Falsa Religião e a Amizade Enganadora—o livro de Jó*. São Paulo: Paulus, 2005.
———. *Messianismo e Modernidade*. São Paulo: Paulus, 2002.
Sassen, Saskia. *As cidades na economia mundial*. São Paulo: Nobel, 1984.

Bibliography

Schipani, Daniel S. *Conscientizacion and Creativity.* Lanham, MD: University Press of America, 1984.

Schokel, Luis A. *Job.* Madrid: Cristandade, 1983.

Schokel, Luis A., and José L. S Díaz. *Job: comentario teológico y literario.* Madrid: Cristandad, 2002.

Shepard, David. *Built as a City: God and Urban World Today.* London: Hodder and Stoughton, 1994.

Sider, Ronald J. *Rich Christians in an Age of Hunger.* Nashville: Nelson, 2005.

Simon, A. *How Much is Enough? Hungering for God in an Affluent Culture.* Grand Rapids: Baker, 2003.

Solle, Dorothe. *Sufrimiento.* Salamanca, Spain: Sígueme, 1988.

Souza, E. C. B., and M. D. B. Magalhães. "Os Pentecostais: entre a fé e a política." *Revista Brasileira de História* 22.43 (2002) 85–105.

Stackhouse, Max L, et al. *The Local Church in a Global Era: Reflections for a New Century.* Grand Rapids: Eerdmans, 2000.

Sung, Jung Mo. *Desejo, Mercado e Religião.* Petrópolis, Brazil: Vozes, 1998.

Ternay, Henry. *O livro de Jó.* Petrópolis, Brazil: Vozes, 2001.

Tournier, Paul. *Culpa e Graça.* São Paulo: ABU, 1985.

Tunnermann, R. *As reformas de Neemias: a reconstrução de Jerusalém e a reorganização de Judá no período Persa.* São Paulo: Paulus, 2001.

Ward, Pete. *Liquid Church.* Carlisle, UK: Paternoster, 2003.

Weaver, J. *Having a Mary Heart in a Martha World.* Colorado: Waterbrook, 2005.

Whybray, Norman. *Job.* Sheffield, UK: Sheffield Academic, 1998.

www.ingramcontent.com/pod-product-compliance
Lightning Source LLC
Chambersburg PA
CBHW071502160426
43195CB00013B/2183